First published in 2005 by New Holland Publishers (UK) Ltd
London • Cape Town • Sydney • Auckland
Garfield House, 86–88 Edgware Road, London W2 2EA, United Kingdom
www.newhollandpublishers.com
80 McKenzie Street, Cape Town 8001, South Africa
14 Aquatic Drive, Frenchs Forest, NSW 2086, Australia
218 Lake Road, Northcote, Auckland

ISBN 1 84330 951 3
10 9 8 7 6 5 4 3 2 1
Editorial Direction: Rosemary Wilkinson Senior Editor: Clare Hubbard Production: Hazel Kirkman
Designed and created for New Holland by AG&G Books Copyright © 2004 "Specialist" AG&G Books
Design: Glyn Bridgewater Illustrations: Dawn Brend, Gill Bridgewater, and Coral Mula
Editor: Alison Copland Photographs: see page 80
Reproduction by Pica Digital Pte Ltd, Singapore
Printed and bound in Malaysia by Times Offset (M) Sdn. Bhd.

The information in this book is true and complete to the best of our knowledge. All recommendations
are made without guarantee on the part of the authors and the publishers. The authors and publishers
disclaim any liability for damages or injury resulting from the use of this information.

Distributed in the US and Canada by: Sterling Publishing Co., Inc., 387 Park Avenue South, New York, NY
10016-8810

The CONTAINER Specialist

The essential guide to planting in containers and designing, improving, and maintaining container gardens

David Squire
Series editors: A. & G. Bridgewater

NH NEW HOLLAND

Contents

Author's foreword 2

GETTING STARTED
Growing plants in containers 3
Range of containers 4
Range of plants for containers 6
Positioning and using containers 8
Seasonal displays 10
Contrasts and harmonies 12
Creating a scented patio 14

PLANTS FOR CONTAINERS
Summer-flowering bedding plants 16
Spring-flowering bedding plants 22
Hardy border perennials 24
Flowering shrubs 30
Foliage shrubs 32
Dwarf and slow-growing conifers 34
Bamboos 36
Bonsai for patios 37
Bulbous plants 38
Culinary herbs for patios 40
Climbing plants 42
Plants for lobbies and porches 44
Growing vegetables in containers 46
Growing fruit in containers 48

PLANTING AND USING CONTAINERS
Choosing and buying plants 50
Window boxes 52
Hanging-baskets 54
Baskets in lobbies and porches 56
Wall-baskets and mangers 58
Stone, glazed, and hypertufa sinks 60
Troughs and planters 62
Raised beds 63
Pots, tubs, and urns 64
Container water features 66
Growing-bags on patios 68
Planting pockets and shelves 69
Wheelbarrows 70
Barrels and casks 71

LOOKING AFTER CONTAINERS
Caring for container plants 72
Winter protection 74
Fixing brackets and hooks 75
Pests and diseases 76

Glossary 78 Index 79

Author's foreword

Growing plants in containers has never been more popular and has enabled many people—often without a garden and perhaps with only a balcony, courtyard, or small patio—to garden and derive enjoyment from growing plants. It has also made gardening possible for wheelchair gardeners and other people who are not as active as they were in earlier years.

The range of containers for plants is wide and encompasses window boxes and hanging-baskets, perhaps the most popular and visually exciting ways to grow plants in containers. Wall-baskets, mangers, tubs, urns, and Versailles planters are other popular containers, as well as growing-bags for vegetables, herbs, spring bulbs, and summer-flowering bedding plants.

There is almost no end to the range of containers and plants; strawberries in planters and barrels, apple trees in tubs and large terra cotta pots, pouches hanging from walls and fences and packed with floriferous summer-flowering trailing and cascading plants, wheelbarrows burgeoning with summer flowers, and stone sinks decked in miniature conifers, alpines, and diminutive bulbs; they are all part of the passion for gardening in containers.

This inspirational all-color book guides novice gardeners through the "getting started" stage of container gardening, as well as providing exciting yet practical ideas for developing their hobby. If you love plants and aspire to creating a container garden, this is an exciting book to have at your elbow.

SEASONS

Throughout this book, advice is given about seasonal tasks. Because of global and even regional variations in climate and temperature, the four main seasons have been used, with each subdivided into "early," "mid-," and "late" —for example, early spring, mid-spring, and late spring. These 12 divisions of the year can be applied to the appropriate calendar months in your local area, if you find this helps.

Growing plants in containers

A popular way to grow plants is to plant them in a wide range of attractive containers and place these on patios and terraces, as well as in courtyards and many other places in a garden. Containers range from hanging-baskets and window boxes, which bring color at waist or head height, to others for placing on the ground or even decorating balconies, edges of garage roofs, porches, and verandas. Some can be used to decorate the sides of steps.

What is container gardening?

CONTAINERS IN GARDENS

- The range of containers used in gardens is wide and many are illustrated and described on pages 4–5. Some are used for single-season plants, such as summer-flowering bedding plants, while others create homes for all-season plants like small shrubs, trees, and conifers.
- Do not confuse "growing plants in containers" in your garden with buying "container-grown" plants from garden centers. Container-grown plants are removed from their containers and planted in garden soil. Alternatively, they can be planted into decorative containers.

WHY GROW PLANTS IN CONTAINERS?

There are both advantages and disadvantages to growing plants in containers and here are a few of them.

Advantages:
- Plants can be positioned where you want them—often near to a house so that they can be easily seen.
- Fragrant plants are readily appreciated.
- Changes can be made from one season to another.
- Success does not depend on the quality of garden soil—it may be infested by pests and diseases.

Disadvantages:
- Plants need regular watering, especially in summer and where the amount of compost is small.
- Regular care and attention is essential for many plants.
- Range of plants is limited to those that flourish in small amounts of compost.

Water features

Miniature ponds in stone sinks and wooden tubs are possible on a patio (see page 66).

Pebble ponds where fountains spray water over pebbles in a shallow base—these are ideal features where toddlers live because, at worst, they only get wet.

Hanging-baskets help to create interest above ground level.

Balcony gardening

Container gardening is ideal for balconies. Here are some ideas.

- Troughs placed on a balcony floor, with trailing stems and flowers cascading outward over the floor.
- Pots, filled with brightly colored summer-flowering plants, securely fixed to the tops of decorative balustrades.
- Tubs of slightly tender plants that can be taken indoors in winter yet still give a good balcony display. Cordylines and Agaves, as well as Yuccas, are excellent plants to use.

Floriferous begonias introduce a medley of bright flowers to containers throughout the summer months.

Range of containers

What sort of container?

Many types of containers can be used, but essentially they need to hold enough compost to support plants, create a firm base, be attractive, and harmonize with their surroundings. Formal containers are ideal for neat and clinical gardens, while rustic types are better for rural gardens that exude a relaxed and easy-going atmosphere. Good construction materials include wood, metal, glass-fiber, plastic, and reconstituted stone—and even redundant car tires!

KEEPING COOL!

Some container materials, such as wood, are slow to warm up in summer as well as providing insulation for soil and roots during cold winters. Others, like thin plastic and metal, warm up rapidly in summer and soon heat up the compost. Glass-fiber is less heat-conductive, while earthenware and reconstituted stone containers keep roots cool in summer.

CONTAINER OPTIONS

Window boxes

Several materials are used in window-box construction.
- **Wood is ideal** and can be tailored to fit most windowsills, although not in excess of 2½ feet long. Preferably use a wooden window box as an outer container, with a 2-foot long, 8-inch wide, and 8-inch deep plastic trough-like box inside it, which can be changed from one season to another.
- **Plastic window boxes** are durable if thick and rigid, but become brittle. They are therefore best used as an inner container. Strong sunlight often degrades them.
- **Terra cotta has** a color and texture that harmonizes with plants. If knocked, terra cotta cracks.
- **Reconstituted stone** is an attractive feature, but is too heavy except for positioning on concrete window sills.
- **Glass-fiber** is long-lived and often used to imitate lead and other metals. If dropped, it is likely to crack.
- **Ornate-textured metal window boxes** are sometimes available. They warm up quickly in summer and are best used in conjunction with an inner plastic container.

↗ Window boxes packed with colorful, scented plants bring color and fragrance to a house as well as a patio.

Hanging-baskets

Several materials are used to make hanging-baskets.
- **Wire-framed baskets** are popular and made in several sizes, from 10 inches to 18 inches wide. Most are coated in plastic to prevent corrosion and to ensure a long, attractive life.
- **Plastic hanging-baskets** help to prevent compost drying out rapidly. They are available in several colors. Those with drip-tray built into their bases are ideal for positioning in lobbies and porches, where water dripping from a basket's base would be a problem. There are several designs, in various widths and depths to suit many different positions.
- **Basket lining materials** are essential for wire-framed baskets. Sphagnum moss is a traditional lining material, but now proprietary liners as well as black polyethylene are popular. Some liners help to conserve moisture in the basket.

↗ Hanging-baskets are a marvelous way to enjoy eye-height color all through the summer.

Troughs

The shape and proportions of troughs roughly resemble those of window boxes, but because they are positioned on the ground troughs can be larger and so accommodate bigger plants. These decorative containers are ideal for a few culinary herbs placed near a kitchen door.
- **Glass-fiber** is strong and can be given an ornate metal appearance. It is best used for relatively small troughs.
- **Reconstituted stone** troughs are often large and decorative, with an informal and relaxed surface. They are expensive to buy.
- **Wooden** troughs are good for rustic settings and are made either of planks of wood or sections of bark.
- **Terra-cotta** troughs are ideal for positioning at the edge of a patio or terrace, or alongside a house wall and in conjunction with pots and tubs. Terra-cotta containers are quite vulnerable to knocks.
- **Plastic** troughs are short-lived containers and look best when trailing stems and flowers cloak their sides.

FURTHER CONTAINER OPTIONS

Tubs, pots, and urns

These have varied uses, as well as differing materials in their construction.

- **Wooden tubs** are good for relaxed and informal displays. Make sure that drainage holes are drilled in the base, and each tub stands on 3–4 bricks.
- **Versailles planters** (square, box-like containers) are usually made of wood, but some are glass-fiber.
- **Jardinières** were traditionally made of lead, but nowadays these are replicated in glass-fiber.
- **Concrete containers**, perhaps shallow and cone-shaped, are popular but are not suitable for rustic settings. Because their sides and base are thick, they are difficult to move.
- **Earthenware pots** and tubs have a natural appearance and are ideal for many types of plant.
- **Reconstituted stone urns** are distinctive and ideal for summer flowers and other seasonal plants.

Cut-out planters

Some containers have cupped openings in their sides in which plants such as herbs, strawberries, and bulbs can be planted. Many home-constructed containers, such as small barrels with windows cut in their sides, are ideal for summer-flowering plants or even longer-lived types such as *Sempervivum* (Houseleeks), which produce masses of evergreen rosettes.

Good drainage is essential in these containers, especially for herbs and strawberries that remain in the container for several years.

↗ *Strawberries grown in planters look good, and taste better than store ones.*

↗ *For an original display, use a small barrel with a window cut out of one side.*

Found items

Many lofts and garden sheds harbor attractive artifacts that can be dusted off and used as containers for plants. These range from metal teapots and kettles to discarded watering-cans and old chimney pots. Some of these can be used alone, while others look good when modified with another container.

← *Plants in small and decorative containers need regular care.*
→ *Try mixing-and-matching containers by placing a hanging-basket on top of a wide, old chimney pot.*

GROWING-BAGS ON PATIOS

Growing-bags are inexpensive to buy yet are able to bring masses of color and interest to patios.

- **Grow tomatoes** in growing-bags, using bamboo canes or proprietary structures to support the plants.
- **Plant growing-bags in the fall** with spring-flowering bulbs. It is possible to reuse growing-bags earlier used for tomatoes; top up with peat.
- **Place growing-bags** with trailing summer-flowering bedding plants along the edges of flat-roofed garages.

MINIATURE WATER GARDENS IN CONTAINERS

An old, deep, stone sink enables the creation of a miniature water garden on a patio. Wooden tubs can also be used. Include only miniature water plants.

Miniature water gardens are ideal for patios and small gardens.

Small containers are summer-only homes for miniature water plants. Move them into a greenhouse or conservatory in winter.

Range of plants for containers

Which plants suit containers?

Good plants for containers range from summer- and spring-flowering bedding plants to small shrubs, trees, and conifers. Bamboos, as well as herbs, vegetables, and fruit, are other possibilities. Small alpine plants in stone sinks create choice features, as well as miniature water plants in tubs or deep stone sinks. Displayed on these pages is a parade of plants for growing in containers, many of which are sure to capture your imagination.

GROWING PLANTS IN CONTAINERS

The central problem in growing plants in containers is the limited amount of compost available to them to create stability as well as supplying water and nutrients. Additionally, because containers are exposed and, perhaps, positioned on window sills, at the edges of balconies, and on tops of walls, they are vulnerable to buffeting wind, strong sunlight during summer and freezing weather in winter. Nevertheless, container-gardening enthusiasts never fail to reveal dedication to their art and invariably clothe their gardens in color throughout the year. It is also an ideal way to grow plants in small gardens.

FRUIT IN CONTAINERS

Strawberries in barrels or strawberry pots are popular—they are easy to grow and the same plants will produce fruits over several years. Apples grown on dwarfing rootstocks, such as M27 and M9, can be grown in large pots.

Summer-flowering bedding plants

These are widely grown during summer in pots, tubs, troughs, window boxes, and hanging-baskets.

- It is possible to raise plants yourself from seeds sown in gentle warmth in late winter or early spring, then grown and slowly acclimatized to outdoor conditions for planting in late spring or early summer (depending on the weather and your area).

- It is also possible to buy young plants and to plant them directly into containers.

Hardy border plants

These plants can be left in tubs or large pots for several years until congested and need to be removed and divided.

- Some of these plants are herbaceous, and others retain some or all of their leaves throughout the winter.

- Buy healthy, well-established plants and, preferably, plant them in spring or early summer.

- Border plants such as Hostas, which are vulnerable to slugs and snails, are given slight protection from these pests.

Small shrubs

Both flowering and foliage shrubs can be grown in tubs and large pots. Later, they can be moved into a garden.

- Flowering shrubs are seasonal and, while some flower in spring, others have flowers in summer.

- Evergreen shrubs—especially the variegated types—create attractive features right through the year.

- Architectural shrubs, such as Yuccas, are ideal for a Mediterranean garden or for a formal one where sharp, clinical lines are desired.

Small trees

Small trees are possible candidates for tubs, especially if low-growing and not creating a major barrier for strong wind in winter, when their roots could be rocked and loosened in the compost.

- The beautiful deciduous shrub *Acer palmatum* 'Dissectum Atropurpureum' forms a low canopy of deeply dissected, bronze-red leaves throughout summer.

- *Acer palmatum* 'Dissectum' is closely related and similarly shaped, with finely dissected green leaves.

Bulbs

Winter-, spring-, and early-summer-flowering bulbs are ideal for containers. With their reserve of food, bulbs are some of nature's best-equipped plants for creating color.

- Miniature winter- and spring-flowering types are best reserved for planting in sink gardens, where they combine well with small rock-garden plants.

- Early spring-flowering bulbs such as Daffodils burst into life and drench containers with color.

Herbs

Many culinary herbs can be grown in containers. While Bay, with its tall and stately appearance, is ideal for tubs or large pots, small herbs are better in pots and planters.

- Try a medley of Chives, Thyme, and Sage in a planter with cupped holes in its sides.

- Plant Mint in individual pots in order to constrain its invasive nature.

- Sow Parsley in small, ornate containers that will perfectly set off the densely curled, mid-green leaves.

Climbers

Climbers introduce vertical color—some live for only one year while others survive from one year to another.

- Plant a large-flowered Clematis in a large pot and let it spread over ornate railings.

- Plant young Sweet Pea plants in large pots in early summer—they will create color throughout the summer.

- Plant a tub with *Humulus lupulus* 'Aureus' (Yellow-leaved Hop); support it with a 5-foot high wigwam of garden canes.

Bamboos

Several bamboos are ideal for planting in tubs or large pots. They are superb for positioning in a Japanese garden.

- Plant small bamboos in large pots and taller ones in wooden tubs or square boxes.

- Stand the container out of direct sunlight and away from strong drafts.

- When plants become congested, in late spring either repot into a larger container or remove, divide and repot into 2–3 pots.

Vegetables

Many vegetables that have fibrous or shallow roots can be grown successfully in containers.

- Early potatoes are possible in large pots and growing-bags. Proprietary potato-growing containers are available.

- Tomatoes are popular for planting in pots and positioning on a warm, sheltered patio.

- Lettuces are ideal for growing in growing-bags and placing on a patio—but only where slugs and snails cannot reach them.

Water-garden plants

These can be created in tubs or deep, stone sinks. Wooden tubs are better than stone sinks as they insulate the water from temperature extremes.

- Miniature, non-invasive aquatic plants are ideal and these include *Carex elata* 'Aurea' (also known as *Carex stricta* 'Bowles Golden'), *Typha minima,* and *Schoenoplectus lacustris* subsp. *tabernaemontani* 'Zebrinus' (also known as *Scirpus zebrinus* and commonly as Zebra Rush) with quill-like stems banded in white and green.

Lobbies and porches

Lobbies and porches are ideal for the hardier houseplants and many are superb when planted in hanging-baskets. However, none of them will survive frost-like conditions.

- There are several suitable fern-like houseplants for this purpose, such as *Asplenium bulbiferum* (Mother Fern) and *Asparagus densiflorus* (Asparagus Fern).

- The flowering *Campanula isophylla* (Italian Bellflower) is moderately hardy, with star-shaped blue flowers in summer.

Dwarf conifers

Dwarf and slow-growing conifers are ideal for creating shape and color interest throughout the year, whether in tubs or large pots, or grouped together in a large trough.

- Position conifers out of strong, direct, or blustery wind, which is a danger to them.

- In windy areas, plant conifers in heavy containers that give them a firm base— and use loam-based compost.

- Make sure the compost is neither too dry in summer nor too wet in winter.

Positioning and using containers

Some containers can be put in many different and imaginative positions on a patio, around a house, or in a garden. They can be used to highlight features such as patio windows, porches, and flights of steps, as well as directing foot traffic away from open casement windows. They are also ideal for creating focal points within a garden. Window boxes are dedicated solely to window sills, but they are still an essential part of the art of container gardening.

WINDOW BOXES FOR ALL SEASONS

Window boxes are superb for brightening windows throughout the year. As soon as a spring display ends, a summer-flowering one can be put in its place. When, in autumn, that fades, a winter display can be ready to take its place. Positioning window boxes needs care. For sash windows (where two frameworks of glass are raised and lowered vertically) a window box can be placed on the sill. For casement windows (which are hinged at their outer edges and open over the sill) window boxes are best placed on strong brackets attached below the window.

Tubs and pots

Groups of tubs and pots create attractive features on patios and terraces, either grouped in small clusters in a sheltered corner or near a patio or kitchen door.

- **When in small groups**, plants afford each other slight protection from strong, gusty winds, as well as creating a mini-environment that is slightly more humid.

- **By using pots** singly or in small groups, the tops of flights of steps can be made more decorative. Use low plants at the top, and taller ones (perhaps upright conifers with colorful foliage) at the base.

Troughs

Troughs are versatile containers and create captivating displays on their own or with groups of pots.

- **Small troughs are ideal** for brightening the edges of patios at ground level or, with the aid of metal supports, fitted to the tops of balustrades.

- **A decorative trough**, with a pot on either side burgeoning with flowers, looks good when placed in front of a window. Leave space between the window and the trough, so that watering and maintenance can be carried out easily.

Mangers and wall-baskets

Mangers and wall-baskets create magnificent display containers against walls. Mangers are 12–28 inches wide, while wire-framed wall-baskets are 9–20 inches across.

- **Large mangers** are excellent for positioning under windows, while small ones are better on walls that are bare and need brightening.

- **Use mangers and wall-baskets** in combinations with troughs and plants in pots.

- **Position wall-baskets** on balcony walls, perhaps on either side of a door. Ensure the door opens freely.

Tubs

Tubs, as well as square and box-like containers, are ideal for shrubs and small trees. They create eye-catching features.

- **Use two large containers** and plant a half-standard *Laurus nobilis* (Bay) tree in each of them. Position them on either side of an entrance. Full standard trees can be used, but usually they are too dominant and certainly more susceptible to damage from strong wind.

- **Round tubs** offer informality and are suitable for a dome-topped shrub or small tree.

Miniature water gardens

Position miniature water gardens in slight or variable shade to ensure that the water does not become excessively warm. Also, avoid overhanging trees.

- **Position the water feature** where it can be easily looked after each day. At the height of summer the water will require regular topping up to compensate for evaporation.

- **A grouping of** a miniature water garden and an old, shallow, stone sink planted with small rock-garden plants and miniature bulbs never fails to attract attention from passers-by.

Growing-bags

Growing-bags are more versatile and economical than most other containers—although not always as pleasing to the eye.

- **Tomatoes, lettuces,** and other vegetables are popular candidates for growing-bags. Position them in good light, with shelter from cold winds in early summer.

- **Plant them with** low-growing culinary herbs and place them near a kitchen door.

- **To produce flowers** for indoor decoration, plant with self-supporting bedding plants. Set in an out-of-the-way position.

Herb pots and planters

Herb planters are ideal for positioning on patios and near kitchen doors. Herbs can also be grown in pots, and these are best displayed in small clusters or in combination with the herb planter.

- **Herb planters,** with their informal appearance, are ideal for rustic patios perhaps surfaced with old stone slabs and with gaps left between them for small plants such as Thyme.

- **Try positioning** a herb planter on a paving slab at the end of a flower border.

Hanging-baskets

Hanging-baskets are versatile and can be used in many exciting and colorful ways. Here are a few display situations to consider.

- **Use two baskets** on either side of a window. Position them so that the edges of the display slightly intrude on the window frame.

- **Suspend a few** hanging-baskets along the edge of a veranda.

- **The ends of carports** benefit from color, but ensure that you will not bump into the baskets.

- **Dull and bland courtyard walls** are soon brightened by the addition of a hanging-basket.

Sink gardens

Shallow stone sinks have an informal presence that harmonizes with relaxed and cottage-garden settings.

- **If you have several** sink gardens, position them at different heights. Four pillars of ornate but structurally sound bricks will make plants easier to admire—and look after.

- **Gardeners in wheelchairs** appreciate raised but stable sink gardens.

- **A sink garden** can be positioned to direct foot traffic, perhaps away from the corner of a building or a window.

Wheelbarrows

When drenched with brightly colored, summer-flowering plants, a wheelbarrow can become a center of attention—a focal point for a patio or a front garden.

- **Always put a wheelbarrow** in place before filling it with plants. When full of potting compost and plants—and well watered—the weight may prevent the barrow being safely moved without the risk of it collapsing.

- **Position the barrow** with its front end attractively angled toward the main viewing area.

Seasonal displays

Color through the year?

By using seasonal arrangements of plants in window boxes it is possible to create color throughout the year. Hanging-baskets are mostly used for displays in summer, while wall-baskets and mangers are ideal for both spring and summer. Tubs usually hold perennial plants such as small shrubs, trees, and conifers, and these remain attractive for several years. Sink gardens are best in spring and early summer, and miniature water gardens throughout summer.

GETTING THE MOST COLOR AND INTEREST

The smaller the garden, the more difficult it is to create interest in borders throughout the year. However, by using containers it is possible to produce color in every season, including winter.

Window boxes can have a yearly cycle of three different seasonal displays, so they are superb for outdoor viewing as well as from indoors. See page 53 for the philosophy of using window boxes in this way.

Hanging-baskets displayed outdoors bring only summer color, but when planted with resilient indoor plants can be placed in a lobby or porch for year-round interest.

Wall-baskets and mangers can be planted with bulbs and biennial plants in the fall and, when the display is over in late spring or early summer, replanted with summer-flowering bedding plants.

SEASONS

Throughout this book, advice is given about seasonal tasks. Because of global and even regional variations in climate and temperature (even within a distance of 100 miles, the arrival of spring can vary by a week or more), the four main seasons have been used, with each subdivided into "early," "mid-," and "late"—for example, early spring, mid-spring, and late spring. These 12 divisions of the year can be applied to the appropriate calendar months in your local area, if you find this helps.

SPRING DISPLAYS

Window boxes

The range of spring-flowering plants—from bulbs to hardy biennials—is wide. Here are two arrangements that create exciting displays.
Medley display (biennials and bulbs): double *Bellis perennis* (English Daisy), *Myosotis* (Forget-me-not), *Muscari armeniacum* (Grape Hyacinth), *Tulipa greigii* (Greig Tulip), *Tulipa fosteriana* (Foster Tulip), and *Erysimum cheiri* (Wallflower).

Medley display (mainly bulbs, plus Polyanthus): *Hyacinthus orientalis* (Hyacinth), *Iris danfordiae* and *Iris reticulata* (Miniature Irises), *Narcissus* (Miniature Trumpet Daffodils), *Primula polyantha* (Polyanthus), and *Tulipa greigii* (Greig Tulip).

Color in troughs

Troughs positioned at ground level and in a wind-sheltered position near to a house or patio wall are ideal for Trumpet-Flowered Daffodils in spring. However, if exposed to blustery spring wind, the flowers and stems can soon be damaged. A trough that can be seen and admired from kitchen or living-room windows is a bonus.

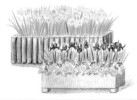

Color in tubs

Tubs are more suitable than troughs for dominant displays in spring. In the fall, plant a mixture of Single Early Tulips and Hyacinths. The Tulips grow 12–15 inches high and in a wide color range. Hyacinths are shorter and in colors that include white, pink, red, and blue. For extra color and to soften the tub's sides, plant variegated small-leaved Ivies around the edges.

Growing-bags

In the fall, after growing a few tomato plants, remove all plant debris, top up with moist peat, and plant a selection of spring-flowering bulbs. Water well and place the growing-bag in a cool area. In spring the bulbs will burst into flower.

SUMMER DISPLAYS

Hanging-baskets

To many container-gardening enthusiasts, hanging-baskets are the best way to introduce summer color on a patio and around a house. As they create color at eye height, any blemishes that arise throughout the summer are soon noticed. Here are a few tips:

- Don't cram in too many plants. Once established, fewer but bigger and healthier plants will look better than masses of starved plants.
- Don't use too many different types of plant. A basket planted with a dozen different plants will not look as effective as 12 plants of only 4–5 different kinds.

Window boxes

The range of plants for summer-flowering window boxes is wide; some are upright and bushy, while others trail and help to cloak the sides of the container. Here are two medleys of plants to consider.

Medley display (mainly flowers): summer-flowering *Viola* x *wittrockiana* (Pansies), *Lobularia maritima* (Sweet Alyssum; also known as *Alyssum maritimum*), *Lobelia erinus* (Edging Lobelia), *Begonia* x *tuberhybrida* (Tuberous-Rooted Begonia), and Zonal Pelargonium.

Medley display (flowers and foliage): *Bassia scoparia* 'Trichophylla' (Burning Bush; also known as *Kochia scoparia* 'Trichophylla'), *Impatiens* (Patience Plant), Godetia, *Lysimachia nummularia* (Creeping Jenny), and *Lobelia erinus* (Edging Lobelia).

↗ *A combination of bushy and trailing plants is essential in a well-balanced box.*

Decorative pots

↗ *Fancy pots in a mixture of sizes and shapes create exciting features on patios and terraces. Some can have a single-color theme, and others a medley of hues. Baskets with a plant pot inside introduce a rural variation to the display.*

WINTER DISPLAYS

Window boxes

Winter displays in window boxes mainly rely on small evergreen shrubs, with variegated trailing plants to soften the edges of the box. Some shrubs, when small, are used for one season and later planted into a larger tub or garden. Because winter-flowering window boxes are usually replanted each autumn, it is an opportunity to try a wide range of plants. Here are a few types to consider. **Berried shrubs:** choose small, heavily berried plants. **Dwarf conifers:** the range is wide and in many attractive colors. **Evergreen shrubs:** these range from the variegated *Aucuba japonica* 'Variegata' to all-green types such as *Gaultheria procumbens*. **Flowering shrubs:** these are more limited than evergreen types, but include winter-flowering *Erica* (Heaths). **Hedera helix (small-leaved variegated Ivies):** many colorful varieties are available.

Tubs

↘ Juniperus horizontalis *'Wiltonii'* (Wilton Carpet Juniper) is slow-growing and carpet-forming, 6–8 inches high and spreading to about 3½ feet wide in six years. However, when small it creates an attractive feature with its bright blue, dense foliage. It needs a wide container, such as a tub, so that it can spread.

↙ Chamaecyparis lawsoniana *'Elwoodii'* is a slow-growing conifer that eventually reaches 6 feet high, but when small is ideal for planting in a window box. It is packed with dark green leaves. An alternative is 'Ellwood's Golden Pillar', with golden-yellow foliage.

← Several Skimmias have berries that persist into winter. Their bright berries create further variation in a pot on a patio. Position them toward the center of the container to give them protection from birds, which soon decimate plants.

Contrasts and harmonies

Producing attractive color harmonies and contrasts is just a matter of selecting plants that suit their backgrounds. On these pages a wide range of plants is suggested that will suit white, gray-stone, red-brick, or dark walls, in both spring and summer seasons. Some of these displays create striking contrasts that soon capture people's attention, while others produce warm and subtle harmonies between plants and their background.

How do I create good color combinations?

INFLUENCE OF GREEN

Green is the most common color in a garden and the surface texture of a leaf strongly influences its perceived color.

- A smooth-surfaced leaf reflects light at the same angle at which the light hits it, making the light purer in color than the same light reflected from a matt surface.
- In nature, few plant surfaces are as smooth as glass, and the scattering of reflected light occurs on the surfaces of most leaves.

CHANGING LIGHT

Throughout the day the intensity of light varies, influencing its perception.

- Pale colors are the first to become discernible in the morning light, as well as the last to be seen in the evening and at dusk.
- Conversely, dark colors such as dark reds and purples are usually the last colors to be seen in the morning, and the first to fade at dusk.

Light, bright colors remain noticeable even into the late evening.

WHITE BACKGROUNDS

Spring displays

White backgrounds are ideal for highlighting yellow, gold, red, scarlet, and dark blue flowers, as well as green foliage which acts as a neutral color. Choose combinations such as:
- *Myosotis* (Forget-me-nots) and golden *Erysimum cheiri* (Wallflowers; also known as *Cheiranthus cheiri*). • double *Bellis perennis* (English Daisies) and red Wallflowers. • blue and red *Hyacinthus orientalis* (Hyacinths) and spring Crocuses, such as the large-flowered hybrids of *Crocus chrysanthus*.

Summer displays

The range of color-contrasting displays is larger in summer than in spring. Choose combinations such as:
- Golden-faced *Tagetes* (Marigolds), dark red *Pelargonium* (Geraniums), and yellow Zinnias. Add the tender *Asparagus densiflorus* 'Sprengeri' (Emerald Fern) to the display. • Trailing red-flowered *Tropaeolum majus* (Nasturtiums) and yellow *Calceolaria* x *herbeohybrida* (Slipperwort) with its pouch-like flowers. Add copious amounts of *Asparagus densiflorus* (Asparagus Fern).

GRAY-STONE BACKGROUNDS

Spring displays

Gray-stone walls enhance and highlight pinks, reds, deep blues, and purples. Choose combinations such as: • For positions in full sun, completely plant the container with red, crimson, and purple or scarlet *Erysimum cheiri* (Wallflowers; also known as *Cheiranthus cheiri*). • Deep blue *Myosotis* (Forget-me-nots) and pink or blue *Hyacinthus orientalis* (Hyacinths). • For a distinctive and clinically shaped display, use just blue *Hyacinthus orientalis* (Hyacinths).

Summer displays

There are many superb flowers that will create distinctive displays. Choose combinations such as: • A medley of deep blue *Lobelia erinus* (Lobelia) and scarlet *Pelargonium* (Geraniums). • Blue-flowered *Campanula isophylla* (Italian Bellflower) and blue *Matthiola incana* (Stocks). • A mixture of Petunias, *Campanula isophylla* (Italian Bellflower), pink-flowered ivy-leaved *Pelargonium* (Geraniums), and dark red *Pelargonium* (Geraniums).

RED-BRICK BACKGROUNDS

Spring displays

Red-brick walls create color-dominant backgrounds that can overwhelm plants unless used in large clusters. Select plants with white, soft blue, silver, and lemon flowers. Silver-leaved plants are also highlighted by red-brick walls. Choose combinations such as: • Light blue *Myosotis* (Forget-me-nots) and white *Hyacinthus orientalis* (Hyacinths). • Bronze and cream *Erysimum cheiri* (Wallflowers; also known as *Cheiranthus cheiri*) and double, white *Bellis perennis* (Daisies).

Summer displays

There are many superb flowers to choose from to create colorful and distinctive displays. Choose combinations such as: • For sunny positions, use a medley of white *Chrysanthemum frutescens* (Marguerites; also known as *Argyranthemum frutescens*), soft-blue Stocks, trailing Lobelia, and the silver-foliaged *Senecio cineraria*. • *Lobularia maritima* (Sweet Alyssum; also known as *Alyssum maritimum*), soft blue Stocks, and the silver-foliaged *Senecio cineraria*.

DARK BACKGROUNDS

Spring displays

Dark backgrounds create strong contrasts for bright and light colors, and are stronger than those produced against red-brick backgrounds. Choose combinations such as: • A dense medley of white or yellow *Hyacinthus orientalis* (Hyacinths). • A strong duo of white *Hyacinthus orientalis* (Hyacinths) and yellow *Crocus chrysanthus* (Crocuses). For added color and to soften the edges of the container, plant variegated small-leaved *Hedera helix* (Ivies).

Summer displays

During summer, there are more plants for creating dramatic contrasts. Choose combinations such as: • Position the yellow-flowered and trailing *Lysimachia nummularia* (Creeping Jenny) close to the edges of the container, with the yellow-flowered *Calceolaria* x *herbeohybrida* (Slipperwort) and dramatically yellow varieties of the tuberous-rooted *Begonia* x *tuberhybrida*. For extra color, use the yellow-leaved form of Creeping Jenny.

WALL-BASKETS

Red and yellow flowers contrast well against white walls.

Pink, red, deep blue, and purple flowers are ideal for gray-stone walls.

White and blue flowers are highlighted by red-brick walls.

Wall-baskets are secured to walls and therefore make contrasts and harmonies between backgrounds and plants readily apparent. Here are a few combinations of plants to consider. **For positioning against white walls:** Use yellow, gold, red, scarlet, and dark blue flowers, as well as green foliage. • Combination of Zinnias, *Pelargonium* (Geraniums), and *Asparagus densiflorus* 'Sprengeri' (Emerald Fern). • Emerald Fern, bright yellow *Calceolaria* x *herbeohybrida* (Slipperwort) and trailing Red Nasturtiums. **For positioning against gray-stone walls:** Use pink, red, deep blue and purple flowers. • Blue-flowered *Campanula isophylla* (Italian Bellflower), Petunias, and *Pelargonium* (Geraniums). • Cascading red or pink Fuchsia, trailing Begonias, and an edging of a variegated *Helichrysum petiolare* (Licorice Plant). **For positioning against red-brick walls:** Use white, soft blue, silver, and lemon flowers, and silver foliage. • White Tulips, blue-flowered *Muscari armeniacum* (Grape Hyacinths) and variegated small-leaved *Hedera helix* (Ivies). • White *Chrysanthemum frutescens* (Marguerites; also known as *Argyranthemum frutescens*), soft blue trailing Lobelias, and blue *Matthiola incana* (Stocks).

INFLUENCE OF COLOR

Blue is associated with calmness and is said to lower blood pressure and to slow up the breathing and pulse rate. A garden that needs to promote a sense of tranquility should be predominantly blue—but not a dark shade.

Yellow is the color of brightness and cheerfulness and is claimed to be the primary color of the intellect, hope, and productivity. Therefore, for a garden that imparts originality of thought and vitality, select yellow-flowered or yellow-leaved plants.

Red is an emotional color and, in contrast to blue, is said to raise blood pressure and increase the rate of respiration. It is also the color of sexual invitation and this, no doubt, accounts for an increased pulse rate.

Green is nature's unifying color and introduces a cool and soothing ambience. It is ideal as a background for other colors and, in containers, to highlight demure shades and suffuse strong colors.

Creating a scented patio

Are there many different fragrances?

The range of fragrances that can be introduced into a garden and containers is wide and includes those as diverse as new-mown hay, parsley, resin, violets, honey, myrrh, and jasmine. However, not all of these fragrances will be produced by plants growing in containers on a patio, and it is possible to add to their scents by planting fragrant climbers in soil alongside a patio and training them over a trellis or against a house wall.

POSITIONING SCENTED CONTAINERS

Containers with scented plants, and when grouped on a warm, sheltered patio, produce concentrated areas of fragrance. Most flowers readily release their fragrance, but some conifers have aromatic foliage that needs to be gently rubbed for it to become apparent. Many small conifers for containers have unusual fragrances, ranging from resinous to warm and sweet. However, some of their scents are reminiscent of soap and paint.

Fragrance in some flowers is immediately noticeable, while for others, such as some Violets, it is initially apparent but after only a few moments disappears completely. Then later it can again be detected. This is only the nose playing tricks.

Hanging-baskets

Hanging-baskets have a limited amount of compost and therefore are best used solely for summer-flowering plants. Nevertheless, there are opportunities to create memorable fragrances.

- *Lobularia maritima*, trailing variety (Sweet Alyssum; also known as *Alyssum maritimum*): new-mown hay redolence. The flowers attract bees, so put the basket where bees will not be a problem.
- Trailing *Tropaeolum majus* (Nasturtiums): faintly scented flowers, with leaves that, when bruised, emit pungency.

Window boxes

There are many plants that create fragrance in window boxes, ranging from small bulbs to miniature conifers and summer bedding plants.

Bulbs:
- *Crocus chrysanthus* (Crocus): sweet.
- *Hyacinthus orientalis* (Hyacinth): strongly sweet.
- *Iris danfordiae*: honey-scented.
- *Iris reticulata*: violet-scented.

Summer-flowering bedding plants:
- Flowering *Nicotiana* (Tobacco Plant): richly sweet.
- *Heliotropium arborescens* (Heliotrope): cherry pie.
- *Viola x wittrockiana* (Pansies): cool and slightly sweet.
- *Lobularia maritima* (Sweet Alyssum; also known as *Alyssum maritimum*): new-mown hay.

Plants in pots

The range of scented plants for tubs is wide and ranges from shrubs to Lilies. Additionally, small conifers can also be used. Some of these plants can also be grown in large pots.

Shrubs:
- *Buxus sempervirens* 'Elegantissima' (Box): pale green, honey-scented flowers.
- *Santolina chamaecyparissus* (Lavender Cotton): camomile fragrant foliage.
- *Rosmarinus officinalis* (Rosemary): rosemary-scented leaves.
- *Salvia officinalis* (Sage): sage-scented leaves.

Wall-baskets

Wall-baskets are ideal for creating centers of strong fragrance, especially from summer-flowering bedding plants (see "Window boxes" opposite). Although fragrant miniature bulbs can be planted in autumn, this often means removing summer-flowering displays before they have completed their full display. If, however, this is not a problem, plant a medley of miniature bulbs, as well as bold and very sweet *Hyacinthus orientalis* (Hyacinths). These are available in several colors, but it is the white ones that usually have the strongest fragrance. Because displays in wall-baskets are regularly changed, miniature and slow-growing conifers are not suitable.

Climbers

Some fragrant climbers can be planted in tubs and large pots and these include the popular Lathyrus odoratus *(Sweet Pea). Fresh plants are raised each year. Other climbers are better suited for planting at the edge of a patio and training against a trellis. Some of these have unusual fragrances, including:*

- *Clematis flammula*: hawthorn-scented.
- *Jasminum officinale*: jasmine-scented.
- *Lonicera americana*: honey-scented.
- *Wisteria*: vanilla-scented.

Troughs

Small troughs that are positioned at ground level can be treated in the same way as window boxes. They are also ideal for planting dwarf and slow-growing conifers. Large troughs can be planted or sown with a wide range of plants, including Evening Stocks and Virginia Stocks (see below). Many Stocks have superb fragrances, including forms of *Matthiola incana*. They are clove-scented and have given rise to Perpetual-flowering Stocks, Brompton Stocks, Ten-week Stocks, and East Lothian Stocks.

EVENING AND NIGHT SCENTS

Where there is space under a window and between a patio, this is ideal for a color and fragrance-packed combination of *Matthiola bicornis* (Evening Stock) and *Malcolmia maritima* (Virginia Stock). They are ideal companions—the Evening Stock provides the fragrance, but has an untidy nature, while the Virginia Stock with its red, lilac, rose, or white flowers provides color. Both are hardy annuals and therefore they can be raised very easily.

- **Evening Stock:** sow seeds ¼ inch deep from early to late spring, where they are to flower. Thin the seedlings to 6–9 inches apart.
- **Virginia Stock:** sow seeds ¼ inch deep from early to late spring, where they are to flower. Thin seedlings to 6 inches apart; plants flower about four weeks after being sown and continue in bloom for up to eight weeks.

Plants in tubs

Many small, scented plants, including Lilies and dwarf conifers, can be grown in tubs on a patio.

Lilies:
- *Lilium auratum* (Golden-rayed Lily): brilliant white and sweetly fragrant.
- *Lilium longiflorum* (Easter Lily): white flowers with a honey-like scent.

Dwarf and slow-growing conifers:
- *Juniperus virginiana* (Eastern Red Cedar): soap and paint redolence.
- *Chamaecyparis obtusa* (Hinoki False Cypress): warm and sweet redolence.
- *Chamaecyparis pisifera* (Sawara False Cypress): resin-like fragrance.

ROSE FRAGRANCES

Several fragrant Roses are ideal for planting alongside a patio to introduce further scents. These include:

- 'Blush Noisette': clove-like scent (Climber).
- 'Constance Spry': myrrh-scented (Shrub Rose or Climber).
- 'The Garland': orange-like scent (Rambler).
- 'Leander': fruity scent (Shrub Rose or Climber).
- 'René André': apple-like scent (Rambler).
- 'Paul Transon': apple-like scent (Rambler).

Summer-flowering bedding plants

Summer-flowering bedding plants are usually half-hardy annuals that are raised in gentle warmth in late winter or early spring, and later, when all risk of frost has passed, planted into containers. Their range is wide, both in color and in style of growth. Some are bushy, whereas others have a cascading or trailing habit that helps to unify the display and soften the edges of containers, especially hanging-baskets and window boxes.

SUMMER-FLOWERING AND FOLIAGE PLANTS

In addition to the many summer-flowering seed-raised bedding plants, there are those grown for their beautiful leaves that help to create greater eye appeal and to highlight flowering types. These include the silver-leaved *Senecio cineraria* 'Silver Dust', *Helichrysum petiolare* (Licorice Plant) and its many variegated and colored-leaf forms, and the yellow-leaved form of *Lysimachia nummularia* 'Aurea' (Creeping Jenny). Other attractively leaved plants include *Pelargonium peltatum* (Ivy-leaved Geraniums) and Zonal Pelargoniums, both of which have the bonus of flowers.

WHEN TO PLANT ...

Half-hardy plants are soon damaged by late spring frost, and therefore are best not planted until all risk of low temperatures has passed. Clearly, this much depends on the area and its vulnerability to late frost, but increasingly the climate is becoming warmer and containers can be planted earlier than several decades ago.

Vulnerable positions:
- Cold, shaded aspects.
- Low-lying positions, perhaps at the base of a slope and where cold air collects.
- At the corners of buildings, where cold air is channeled from one position to another.

THOMPSON & MORGAN

Ageratum houstonianum
Floss Flower (UK/USA)
Pussy-foot (USA)
Height: 5–12 inches
Spread: 6–12 inches
Half-hardy annual, with bluish-mauve flowers. There are many varieties, in bright blue, mauve, pink, and white.

THOMPSON & MORGAN

Anagallis monelli
Blue Pimpernel (UK/USA)
Height: 9 inches
Spread: 9 inches
Half-hardy annual with a neat, compact habit and masses of large, azure-blue flowers from spring to autumn.

THOMPSON & MORGAN

Asarina purpusii 'Victoria Falls'
Height: 5–6 inches
Spread: 6–8 inches
Half-hardy annual with a tumbling mass of cerise-purple flowers with long trumpets. Trails up to 15 inches.

THOMPSON & MORGAN

Asarina x hybrida 'Red Dragon'
Climbing, ideal for baskets, where stems can be supported.
Half-hardy annual, with carmine-red flowers, up to 3 inches long. Plants become drenched in color.

THOMPSON & MORGAN

Begonia semperflorens 'Stara Mixed'
Fibrous Begonia (UK)
Wax Begonia (UK/USA)
Height: 8–10 inches
Spread: 10–12 inches
Half-hardy, branching annual with flowers in white, rose, and scarlet.

Begonia sutherlandii 'Orange Shower'

Trailing

Half-hardy, tuberous-rooted begonia with a cascading nature. Distinctive orange flowers. Ideal for planting in hanging-baskets and wall-baskets.

Begonia x tuberhybrida 'Dragon Wing'

Trailing and bushy

Half-hardy, tuberous-rooted begonia with a cascading nature. Clusters of scarlet-red flowers. Ideal for baskets and containers.

Bidens ferulifera 'Golden Eye'

Height: 8–12 inches

Prostrate and tumbling

Half-hardy annual with beautiful bright yellow flowers that are borne amid fern-like foliage.

Calceolaria integrifolia 'Sunshine'

Pouch Flower (UK/USA)

Slipperwort (USA)

Height: 10–15 inches

Trailing and cascading

Half-hardy shrubby perennial, ideal in a hanging-basket, with yellow flowers.

Calendula officinalis

English Marigold (UK)

Pot Marigold (UK/USA)

Height: 12–15 inches

Spread: 10–12 inches

Hardy annual, often grown in pots, with large, daisy-like, bright yellow or orange flowers. Some forms are dwarf.

Campanula isophylla

Italian Bellflower (UK/USA)

Star of Bethlehem (UK)

Height: 6 inches

Trailing

Hardy perennial, with masses of star-shaped, 1-inch wide, blue, or white flowers.

Cascade Geraniums

(also known as Balcon and Continental Geraniums)

Height: 8–12 inches

Trailing and cascading

Half-hardy annuals which become swamped with masses of flowers in shades of scarlet, salmon, pink, and lilac.

Clematis tangutica 'Radar Love'

Height: 1½–2 feet

Climbing and scrambling

Hardy perennial, raised from seed and flowers three months after sowing. Nodding, rich yellow flowers. Ideal for hanging-baskets.

WHITE AND SILVER THEMES

White- and silver-themed displays have a delicate and demure quality, especially when seen in partial shade.

• When positioned in full sun, a white and silver display becomes more intense and dramatic.

• Flowers in small, clustered heads reflect less light than large ones, and consequently look less dramatic and intensely white.

• In hot countries, where strong sunshine is assured, a white display can be too intense. Therefore, add pale mauve and faintly blue-tinged flowers to reduce the visual strength of the display.

THOMPSON & MORGAN

Datura 'Ballerina Mixed'

Thorn Apple (UK/USA)

Height: 1½–2 feet

Spread: 1½–2 feet

Half-hardy shrub raised from seeds, with upward-facing, primrose-yellow flowers flushed purple or pure white.

THOMPSON & MORGAN

Datura meteloides 'Evening Fragrance'

Thorn Apple (UK/USA)

Height: 14–18 inches

Spread: 14–15 inches

Half-hardy annual that bears large, trumpet-shaped, white and soft lavender, fragrant flowers.

THOMPSON & MORGAN

Eschscholzia maritima prostrata 'Golden Tears'

California Poppy (UK/USA)

Height: 6–9 inches

Spreading and trailing to 2 feet

Hardy annual, usually raised as a half-hardy annual, with golden-yellow flowers amid blue-green leaves.

THOMPSON & MORGAN

Heliotropium arborescens

(syn. *Heliotropium* x *hybridum*)

Cherry Pie (UK) **Heliotrope** (UK/USA)

Height: 15–18 inches

Spread: 12–15 inches

Half-hardy perennial grown as a half-hardy annual. Fragrant flowers in violet, through lavender, to white.

THOMPSON & MORGAN

Impatiens hawkererii New Guinea 'Java Flames Mixed'

Height: 9–12 inches

Spread: 9–12 inches

Half-hardy annual with a compact nature and masses of fluorescent flowers. Ideal for hanging-baskets and other containers.

THOMPSON & MORGAN

Impatiens walleriana 'Unique'

Patience Plant (UK/USA)

Height: 8–10 inches

Spread: 8–12 inches

Half-hardy annual with a medley of single- and bicolored flowers. Colors include white to pink and red.

THOMPSON & MORGAN

Laurentia axillaris Stars Series

Height: 6 inches

Spread: 8–12 inches

Half-hardy annual, initially forming a dome and later spreading with fragrant flowers in blue, pink, or white.

Lobelia erinus—both trailing and compact forms

Edging Lobelia (UK/USA)

Trailing Lobelia (UK/USA)

Height: 4–9 inches

Spread: 4–9 inches—some trail

Half-hardy perennial raised as a half-hardy annual, with blue, white, or red flowers.

Lobularia maritima

(syn. *Alyssum maritimum*)

Sweet Alyssum (UK/USA)

Height: 3–6 inches

Spread: 8–12 inches

Hardy annual usually grown as a half-hardy annual, with a wide color range— white, violet-purple, and deep purple.

Lobularia maritima pendula 'Wandering Star'

(syn. *Alyssum maritimum pendula* 'Wandering Star')

Height: 6 inches

Trailing nature

Half-hardy annual, with fragrant, cream, purple, pink, and rose flowers.

Nicotiana 'Avalon Lime and Purple Bicolor'

Tobacco Plant (UK)

Height: 8–12 inches

Spread: 8–12 inches

Half-hardy annual with a compact nature and large, lime and purple bicolored flowers. Ideal for containers.

Pansy 'Universal Citrus Mixed'

Garden Pansy (UK/USA)

Pansy (UK/USA)

Height: 6–8 inches

Spread: 6–10 inches

Hardy perennial with large, pansy-like flowers in orange, yellow, and white.

Pelargonium 'Regalia'

Height: 9–12 inches

Spread: 12–15 inches

Half-hardy annual with flowers in several individual colors, including deep red, pink, and white. Unlike many Pelargoniums, it is raised from seeds.

Petunia milliflora 'Fantasy'

Height: 8–10 inches

Spread: 10–12 inches

Half-hardy annual with a compact and miniature habit, bearing masses of loose, trumpet-shaped flowers in a wide range of colors.

Petunia 'Prism Sunshine'

Height: 10–12 inches

Spread: 12–15 inches

Half-hardy annual with large, bright yellow flowers that fade to cream and are often veined in lime-green.

Petunia 'Wave Series'

Height: 6–8 inches

Trailing and spreading to 2½ feet

Half-hardy annual with masses of trumpet-shaped flowers; available in single and mixed colors.

Salvia splendens

Scarlet Sage (USA)

Height: 12–15 inches

Spread: 8–10 inches

Half-hardy perennial invariably grown as a half-hardy annual, with spires of scarlet flowers. Ideal in tubs, troughs, and window boxes.

BLUE THEMES

Emotionally, blue creates tranquillity, and for a restful ambience in a garden use this color in hanging-baskets and window boxes, where it can be easily seen. Many blues, however, are not clear and cool but more along the color spectrum toward indigo and violet. Pale shades are more toward mauve and create a restful ambience.

Dark blue hanging-baskets are more dramatic outdoors than light shades, especially when positioned against a white wall. Light blue hanging-baskets are ideal for lobbies and porches, as well as in conservatories where a non-aggressive display is essential if it is to be a social and restful area.

Sanvitalia procumbens 'Irish Eyes'

Height: 4–6 inches

Trailing

Half-hardy annual with masses of golden-yellow, double, and semi-double flowers, each with an attractive eye. It is ideal for planting in hanging-baskets and window boxes, as well as pouches.

Sanvitalia procumbens 'Orange Sprite'

Height: 4–5 inches

Trailing

Half-hardy annual with a profusion of semi-double orange-colored flowers with dark centers. It is ideal for planting in hanging-baskets and window boxes.

Tagetes erecta

African Marigold (UK/USA)

Aztec Marigold (USA)

Height: 2–2½ feet

Spread: 12–18 inches

Half-hardy annual with well-branched stems and lemon-yellow flowers. Other colors range from yellow to orange; some are dwarf.

Tagetes patula

French Marigold (UK/USA)

Height: 12 inches

Spread: 10–12 inches

Half-hardy annual with a bushy nature and yellow or mahogany-red flowers. Single and double-flowered varieties; some have a dwarf nature.

YELLOW THEMES

Yellow is the brightest and most dramatic of all colors and highly visible. It exudes vibrancy and life. However, yellow is a complex color and can include pale cream, demure primrose, and fresh lemon, as well as deepening through old gold to orange and bronze. Few patio-brightening features are totally yellow.

Yellow-themed hanging-baskets and window boxes are ideal for brightening dull areas where perhaps there is a limited amount of light. Use the strongest yellows and largest flowers for such areas, reserving the more delicately shaped yellow flowers for brighter areas.

Thunbergia alata

Black-eyed Susan (UK)

Clockvine (USA)

Height: 4–6 feet—in a pot

Climbing and twining

Half-hardy annual with spectacular, 2-inch wide, orange-yellow flowers with dark centers.

Tropaeolum majus (dwarf)

Common Nasturtium (USA)

Nasturtium (UK)

Height: 15–18 inches

Climbing and trailing

Half-hardy annual with circular leaves and orange or yellow flowers. Plant in a pot or window box; provide supports.

Verbena erinoides 'Lavender Mist'

Verbena (UK/USA)

Vervain (UK)

Height: 10–12 inches

Spread: 10–15 inches

Half-hardy annual with small bunches of pastel-lavender and misty-white flowers.

Verbena x hybrida 'Sandy Mixed'

Verbena (UK/USA)

Vervain (UK)

Height: 8–10 inches

Spread: 8–12 inches

Half-hardy, compact annual; flower colors include white, red, and carmine.

THOMPSON & MORGAN

Viola x hybrida 'Magnifico'
Viola (UK/USA)
Height: 6–8 inches
Spread: 6–8 inches
Half-hardy annual with a compact nature and pure white flowers with violet shading at their edges.

THOMPSON & MORGAN

Viola x hybrida 'Penny Orchid Frost'
Viola (UK/USA)
Height: 4–6 inches
Spread: 6–8 inches
Half-hardy annual with a compact nature and flowers with orchid-like centers and petals with frost-colored edges.

THOMPSON & MORGAN

Viola x wittrockiana 'Flambé Red'
Viola (UK/USA)
Height: 6–9 inches
Spread: 8–10 inches
Hardy perennial, raised from seed and with flowers in pastel shades ranging through rose, flame-red, and ruby.

THOMPSON & MORGAN

Wahlenbergia annularis 'Melton Bicolor'
Rock Bell (UK)
Height: 12–18 inches
Spread: 15–20 inches
Half-hardy annual with masses of white, bell-shaped flowers that change to pale blue or pale violet.

RED AND PINK THEMES

Red is a full-blooded and dramatic color, while pink is a desaturated red with a warm and romantic nature; few people do not find pink to be an attractive color. Strongly red designs dominate their surroundings and nearby plants, while pink displays, although at risk of being dominated by stronger colors, nevertheless are often more memorable.

Use strong reds with great care and in limited amounts. Pink, however, can be used in large amounts and still remain attractive. To create a diffused theme, add some white flowers into a pink-themed basket.

Zinnia elegans
Youth and Old Age (USA)
Height: 6–30 inches
Spread: 6–15 inches
Half-hardy annual with many varieties and colors, including white, purple, yellow, orange, red, and pink. Ideal for window boxes.

OTHER SUMMER-FLOWERING BEDDING PLANTS TO CONSIDER ...

Each year more seed-raised, summer-flowering plants are added to the vast repertoire of plants for growing in containers, and here a few of them.

- *Anagallis linifolia* 'Gentian Blue': blue flowers on plants 6–9 inches high.
- *Antirrhinum pendula multiflora* 'Chinese Lanterns': superb cascading Antirrhinum with a mixture of seven colors, including pure colors, as well as bicolors. Ideal for hanging-baskets and window boxes.
- *Brachycombe iberidifolia* 'Splendor': masses of flowers in blue to purple or white, on plants 9–12 inches high.
- *Campanula carpatica* 'Bellissimo': plants drenched in chalice-shaped blue or white flowers on plants 6 inches high.
- *Gypsophila muralis* 'Gypsy': neat and compact mounds packed with semi- to fully double pink flowers. Ideal for hanging-baskets and other containers.
- *Impatiens walleriana* 'Double Carousel Mixed': spectacular,

double flowers borne on well-branched plants in a wide range of bright colors.

- *Nemophylla maculata*: light blue flowers with a deep blue spot at the tip of each petal, on plants 3–6 inches high, then trailing.
- *Nemophylla menziesii* 'Pennie Black': purple to black flowers, each about ¾ inches wide, on plants 2–4 inches high and then spreading.
- *Nierembergia* 'Mont Blanc': cup-shaped white flowers on plants 4–6 inches high.
- *Silene pendula* 'Peach Blossom': masses of double flowers; deep pink when in bud, opening to salmon and maturing to white. Plants grow to about 4–6 inches high, then cascade.
- *Viola x williamsiana* 'Four Seasons Hybrids': trailing, with sweetly scented small flowers in four individual and different colors—lilac, golden-yellow, purple, and violet.

Spring-flowering bedding plants

How do I grow these plants?

Spring-flowering bedding plants are invariably hardy biennials raised from seed sown during the previous late spring and early summer and planted into containers in late summer or early autumn. They are inexpensive, and once planted need little attention. Spring-flowering bulbs are other container brighteners in spring, and these are discussed on pages 38–39. Many bulbs are ideal companions for spring-flowering bedding plants (see right).

HARDY BIENNIALS AND PERENNIALS

Hardy biennials are ideal spring-flowering bedding plants. The term "biennial" means that a plant is sown and raised one year, and produces flowers during the following season. This is a convenient explanation as to how a plant is raised, but not all plants grown as biennials are really biennial. For example, the popular *Bellis perennis* (English Daisy) is a hardy perennial invariably raised as a biennial. *Myosotis* (Forget-me-nots) are either biennial or short-lived perennials. The Hollyhock is a hardy perennial usually grown as a biennial, and flowers from mid-summer to early autumn.

THOMPSON & MORGAN

Bellis perennis
English Daisy (USA)
Height: 2–4 inches
Spread: 3–4 inches
Bright-faced flowers from early spring to autumn. Many varieties, in white, carmine, pink, salmon, or rich cherry.

Erysimum x allionii
(syn. Cheiranthus x allionii)
Siberian Wallflower (UK)
Height: 12–15 inches
Spread: 10–12 inches
Masses of fragrant, orange flowers in terminal clusters from mid-spring to early summer. Plant in tubs.

Erysimum alpinum
(syn. E. hieraciifolium)
Alpine Wallflower (UK)
Height: 6 inches
Spread: 4–6 inches
In late spring it bears a mass of fragrant, yellow flowers. There are also varieties with mauve and pale yellow flowers.

Erysimum cheiri
Wallflower (UK/USA)
English Wallflower (USA)
Height: 8–12 inches
Spread: 6–8 inches
Fragrant flowers from mid-spring to early summer. Many colors, including orange, blood-red, yellow, and rose-pink.

Myosotis sylvatica
Forget-me-not (UK/USA)
Height: 8–12 inches
Spread: 6 inches
Misty-blue flowers in lax sprays during late spring and into early summer. Varieties in several shades of blue.

Primula x polyantha
Polyanthus (UK/USA)
Height: 6–10 inches
Spread: 6–10 inches
Superb spring plant in a wide color range, including yellow, cream, white, pink, blue, and crimson.

ADDING EVERGREEN TRAILERS ...

Small, trailing plants for adding to spring displays have to survive the rigors of winter, and few plants are more suited for this than variegated small-leaved Ivies. They are ideal for planting at the sides of containers. Their range is wide and includes many varieties of *Hedera helix*, the Common Ivy. Garden centers and nurseries offer a wide range of variegated Ivies, and a few to try include:

- 'Elegance': light green, lobed leaves with uneven silver edges.
- 'Glacier': silver-gray, with narrow, white edges.
- 'Gold Child': leaves edged in yellow.
- 'Goldheart' (also known as 'Oro di Bogliasco'): leaves conspicuously splashed gold at their centers.
- 'Pittsburgh': all-green, five-lobed leaves that create a non-attention-seeking yet attractive frill to tubs.
- 'Sagittifolia Variegata': variegated, deeply lobed green leaves with yellow edges.

ADDING EVERGREEN SHRUBS ...

Several variegated evergreen shrubs when small can be added to spring displays in window boxes and troughs to create extra color. They are especially useful should the weather become exceptionally cold or the wind severe, causing damage to hardy biennials and flowers of bulbous plants. Shrubs to consider include:

- *Euonymus fortunei* 'Emerald 'n' Gold': green leaves brightly variegated in gold. They assume bronzy-pink tones in winter. Eventually a moderately large shrub.
- *Hebe* x *andersoniana* 'Variegata': light green leaves that are dominantly edged and splashed in cream.
- *Aucuba japonica* 'Variegata' (Spotted Laurel): shiny green leaves blotched yellow. Eventually forms a large shrub.

ADDING CONIFERS ...

Positioning conifers in window box and trough displays of spring-flowering bedding plants—perhaps with the addition of bulbs—keeps the display attractive for a longer period.

- Several slow-growing and dwarf conifers are featured on pages 34–35, in colors and shapes that introduce contrasts and harmonies. Position short, bushy types at the ends, so that they cloak the edges. Conversely, put taller and upright conifers toward the center to produce a focal point.
- When slow-growing conifers become too large for the container, plant them in tubs on a patio, or in a garden.

RAISING BIENNIALS

Biennials are inexpensively raised from seeds sown outdoors during late spring and early summer. In preparation:

- If a piece of ground has not been dug in late autumn or early winter as a site reserved for sowing hardy biennials, in early spring dig a piece of ground, removing all weeds.
- In mid-spring, use a garden fork to break down large lumps and a rake to level the surface. Systematically shuffle sideways over the seed bed to uniformly consolidate the soil. Then, rake the surface level.
- Insert 12-inch long sticks 9 inches apart on opposite sides of the seed bed.
- Stretch a garden line between two sticks and use a draw-hoe to form a drill ½ inch deep. Alternatively, use a narrow, straight piece of wood for guidance.
- Tip a few seeds into the palm of a hand and slowly dribble them along the row. Ensure they are not touching and are

evenly spaced. If they fall in clusters, it means that extra thinning will be needed later.

- Use the back of a metal rake to carefully push and draw friable soil over the seeds without disturbing them.
- Firm the soil by using the head of the rake.
- Lightly but thoroughly water the soil, taking care not to disturb the surface unnecessarily.
- Place wire-netting or twiggy sticks over the drills to prevent birds disturbing the seeds.
- When the seedlings are large enough to handle, either thin them out or transfer to a nursery bed. For small plants such as Daisies, thin seedlings to about 4 inches apart; for larger biennials such as Wallflowers thin to 6 inches.
- Transfer the plants to containers in early autumn, especially if the container is also to hold bulbs, which are planted about the same time.

Hardy border perennials

How do I grow these plants?

Border plants are perennial, and last from one season to another, until they become too large for the container and need to be removed, divided, and put into another container or a garden border. Some hardy border perennials have a herbaceous nature—the leaves die down in autumn or early winter and fresh ones appear in spring or early summer. Other border plants will retain their foliage throughout all or most of the year.

LOOKING AFTER BORDER PERENNIALS

These plants usually need little attention, except to remove damaged leaves and dead flowers throughout the season, and to pull or cut off stems and leaves from those plants that die down each year. However, some of these plants—especially Hostas—can be badly damaged by slugs and snails, especially when positioned in slight shade and on damp patios. Pellets and baits help to prevent damage, as well as placing containers—if their size is right—on inverted pots or in wire frames. Alternatively, scattering broken egg shells around pots may deter these pests.

BORDER PERENNIALS IN CONTAINERS

The main difficulty when growing border perennials in containers is to keep the compost moist throughout summer, as well as relatively dry in winter. Compost rich in peat helps to retain moisture, but if it should become dry, it is far more difficult to remoisten. Regularly watering the compost is the main task during hot summers.

In winter, water-saturated compost is likely to freeze and cause damage to roots. Plants that have soft, tuberous roots are most at risk. Covering the surface of the compost with straw helps to keep the compost dry, and thereby prevents it from freezing.

Aegopodium podagraria **'Variegatum'**
Variegated Bishop's Weed (USA)
Variegated Ground Elder (UK/USA)
Height: 6–10 inches
Spread: Forms a clump
Light to mid-green leaves edged in white, even when grown in light shade.

Agapanthus **'Lilliput'**
African Lily (UK/USA)
Height: 18 inches
Spread: 10–12 inches
Narrow, green leaves and upright stems bearing umbrella-like heads of blue flowers during mid- and late summer.

Agave americana **'Variegata'**
Variegated Century Plant (UK/USA)
Height: 2½–3 feet
Spread: 2–2½ feet
Tender succulent with thick, sword-like, gray-green leaves with yellow edges. Needs frost-free winter conditions.

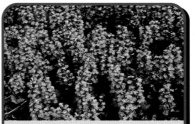

Ajuga reptans
Carpet Bugle (USA)
Height: 4–12 inches
Spread: 12–18 inches
Spreading herbaceous perennial with whorls of blue flowers in early and mid-summer. Several colored-leaf forms.

Alchemilla mollis
Lady's Mantle (UK/USA)
Height: 12–18 inches
Spread: 15–20 inches
Herbaceous perennial that has light green, lobed leaves, and produces masses of sulfur-yellow flowers from early to late summer.

SELECTING SUITABLE PLANTS

Some border perennials are not suited to life in a container, especially when tall and needing support. Here are a few indicators that will help you to choose the right plants:

- Select relatively low-growing plants, especially if your patio is exposed to strong and gusting wind.
- Choose plants that have both interesting flowers and attractive leaves, especially if the flowering period is short. Hostas have the dual role, and there are many from which to choose (see page 26).
- If the leaves remain throughout winter, select plants which have a domed outline and create little resistance to wind. Such plants are also less likely to be damaged by heavy snowfalls, although it is always wise to gently remove snow at the first opportunity.
- Select winter-brightening plants as well as those that reveal their qualities during summer. Winter flowers are always cherished. Frost on the leaves of plants can provide a further winter attraction.

CONTAINER COMPANIONS

Agapanthus in Versailles planters—see below right for plants.

Stachys byzantina in low Ali Baba type pots—see page 29 for plants.

Anthemis punctata subsp. cupaniana
Golden Marguerite (UK/USA)
Height: 6–10 inches
Spread: 12–15 inches
Short-lived herbaceous perennial with bright-faced, daisy-like, yellow-centered white flowers from early to late summer.

Aquilegia McKana Hybrids
Granny's Bonnet (UK)
European Columbine (USA)
Height: 2–2½ feet
Spread: 12–15 inches
Herbaceous perennial with cream, yellow, pink, red, crimson, or blue flowers during late spring and early summer.

Astilbe x arendsii
Height: 1½–2 feet
Spread: 15–20 inches
Hardy herbaceous perennial with feather-like flower plumes in various colors from early to late summer.

Bergenia cordifolia
Elephant's Ears (UK)
Height: 10–12 inches
Spread: 12–15 inches
Hardy border plant with evergreen, rounded leaves and clusters of bell-shaped flowers in early and mid-spring.

Crocosmia x crocosmiiflora
Montbretia (UK/USA)
Height: 1½–2 feet
Spread: Clump-forming
Slightly tender cormous plant for a tub, with funnel-shaped flowers from mid- to late summer, in colors ranging from yellow to deep red.

Dicentra spectabilis
Bleeding Heart (UK/USA)
Height: 18–30 inches
Spread: 18–20 inches
Hardy herbaceous perennial with distinctive, heart-shaped, rose-red, and white flowers during early summer.

OTHER AGAPANTHUS ...

Agapanthus seldom fail to attract attention, and they are ideal plants for a tub or other large container. Their range is wide, and includes:

- *Agapanthus praecox*: a half-hardy perennial, which produces magnificent umbrella-like heads of bright to pale blue flowers. There is also a white-flowered form.
- *Agapanthus* 'Headbourne Hybrids': hardier than species types, with distinctive flowerheads in colors from violet-blue to pale blue.
- *Agapanthus campanulatus* 'Isis': this is a superb plant with a free-flowering habit, producing many heads of deep blue flowers.

Doronicum plantagineum

Leopard's Bane (UK/USA)

Height: 1½–2½ feet

Spread: 15 inches

Hardy herbaceous perennial with large, daisy-like, bright yellow flowers during late spring and early summer.

Epimedium perralderianum

Barrenwort (UK)

Bishop's Hat (UK)

Height: 8–12 inches

Spread: 12–18 inches

Hardy, evergreen perennial with leaves at first bright green, becoming coppery-bronze in autumn. Yellow flowers.

HOSTAS FOR CONTAINERS

The range of Hostas has increased dramatically in recent years and there are many superb plants, including:

- *Hosta sieboldiana*: glossy-green leaves and dull white flowers.
- 'Blue Moon': small, deep blue leaves and grayish-mauve flowers.
- 'Golden Prayers': golden-yellow leaves and mauve flowers.
- 'Shade Fanfare': green leaves with broad, cream edges. The green becomes yellow when the plant is positioned in full sunlight.
- 'Wide Brim': oval, blue-green leaves irregularly edged in cream to golden-yellow. Lavender-colored flowers.

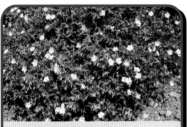

Geranium endressii

Cranesbill (UK/USA)

Height: 12–18 inches

Spread: 15–18 inches

Hardy herbaceous perennial with pale pink flowers from early summer to autumn. Many superb varieties.

Hakonechloa macra 'Aureola'

Height: 10–12 inches

Spread: 2½–3 feet

Hardy, cascading perennial grass with narrow, bright yellow leaves striped green. There are other superb forms.

Helleborus niger

Christmas Rose (UK/USA)

Height: 12–18 inches

Spread: 15–18 inches

Hardy perennial with evergreen leaves. From mid-winter to early spring it bears white, saucer-shaped flowers.

DORONICUMS TO CONSIDER ...

Several superb varieties of this early-summer brightener are ideal for containers. Their strongly yellow flowers soon capture attention, but ensure that they do not dominate plants with demure flowers. Select low-growing types. Varieties to try include:

- 'Harpur Crewe': distinctive, with golden-yellow flowers up to 3 inches wide.
- 'Miss Mason': grows to about 18 inches high, with bright yellow flowers up to 2½ inches wide.
- 'Spring Beauty': grows to about 15 inches high with double, deep-yellow flowers.

Helleborus orientalis

Lenten Rose (UK)

Height: 18–24 inches

Spread: 18 inches

Hardy perennial with evergreen leaves. During late winter and early spring it has cream flowers flecked with crimson.

Hemerocallis thunbergii

Day Lily (UK/USA)

Height: 2½–3 feet

Spread: 2 feet

Hardy herbaceous perennial with large, trumpet-shaped, sulfur-apricot flowers during early and mid-summer.

Heuchera sanguinea
Coral Flower (UK)
Coral Bells (USA)
Height: 12–15 inches
Spread: 12–15 inches
Hardy evergreen herbaceous perennial with small, bright red flowers. 'Alba', with yellow flowers, is shown above.

Hosta fortunei var. albopicta
Plantain Lily (UK/USA)
Height: 15–18 inches
Spread: 18 inches
Hardy herbaceous perennial with pale green leaves variegated buff-yellow. There are many other superb varieties.

Houttuynia cordata 'Chameleon'
Height: 6–10 inches
Spread: Spreading and branching
Hardy herbaceous perennial with leaves that have a patchwork of yellow, green, bronze, and red. Small, white flowers.

Lamium maculatum
Dead Nettle (UK)
Spotted Dead Nettle (USA)
Height: 6–9 inches
Spread: Spreading
Hardy herbaceous perennial with mid-green leaves with a central silver stripe. Pink-purple flowers in late spring.

Liatris spicata
Blazing Star (UK/USA)
Spike Gayfeather (UK/USA)
Height: 2 feet
Spread: 12–18 inches
Hardy, tuberous-rooted herbaceous perennial with spires of pinkish-purple flowers in late summer and into autumn.

Limonium latifolium
Sea Lavender (UK/USA)
Statice (USA)
Height: 1½–2 feet
Spread: 1½ feet
Hardy perennial with leathery, dark green leaves. From mid- to late summer it bears clouds of lavender-blue flowers.

OTHER HEMEROCALLIS TO CONSIDER ...

Many of the colorful *Hemerocallis* hybrids are well worth planting in tubs. These include:
- 'Black Magic': ruby purple with a distinctive yellow throat.
- 'Buzz Bomb': rich velvety-red.
- 'Cartwheels': large, bright yellow flowers that open to create large and nearly flat heads.
- 'Little Wine Cup': dwarf plant, with burgundy flowers; golden throats.
- 'Pink Damask': superb plant, with warm pink flowers that reveal a yellow throat.
- 'Stella D'Oro': dwarf plant, with canary-yellow, bell-shaped flowers with an orange throat.

GERANIUM OR PELARGONIUM?

Geraniums and Pelargoniums are frequently confused with each other, especially as Pelargoniums are popularly known as Geraniums.
- Geraniums are herbaceous perennials grown mainly in gardens but also in tubs and other large containers on patios and terraces. They are hardy and can be left outdoors all year.
- Pelargoniums are warmth-loving shrubs—mainly from southern Africa—that in temperate climates are raised as tender plants for growing in pots, tubs, and other containers. They create magnificent displays outdoors in summer, but are soon killed by low temperatures.

OTHER LAMIUMS TO CONSIDER ...

These are durable perennials and ideal for creating color in tubs. They are often erroneously considered not to be sufficiently attractive for planting in containers, but they thrive in sun or shade. Here are a few to try:
- 'Album': mid-green leaves with a central silver stripe; white flowers.
- 'Aureum': slow-growing, with attractive golden foliage. It is best positioned in full sun in order to encourage the development of bright-colored leaves.
- 'Roseum': mid-green leaves with a central silver stripe; the flowers are shell-pink.

Lysimachia nummularia
Creeping Jenny (UK/USA)
Moneywort (UK/USA)
Height: 2–3 inches
Spread: Trailing to about 1½ feet
Hardy evergreen plant with prostrate stems with mid-green leaves and yellow flowers during early and mid-summer.

Lysimachia nummularia 'Aurea'
Yellow-leaved Moneywort (UK/USA)
Height: 2–3 inches
Spread: Trailing to about 1½ feet
Hardy evergreen plant with prostrate stems, beautiful yellow leaves and yellow flowers in early and mid-summer.

Melissa officinalis 'Aurea'
Golden Balm (UK/USA)
Height: 2½ feet
Spread: 12–18 inches
Hardy herbaceous perennial (it is a form of the well-known Balm) that has golden-green leaves.

GROWING GRASSES IN CONTAINERS

Many grasses are ideal for growing in containers and positioning on patios, terraces, and around houses. Some have a cascading habit that creates an attractive outline and clothes the upper edges of the container. Regular watering is essential to ensure that the relatively small amount of compost does not become dry.

In addition to the superb grass *Hakonechloa macra* 'Aureola' there are other varieties to consider, including 'Alboaurea' with leaves striped off-white and gold; in autumn they assume rich pink and red shades.

There are several grasses that can be used to create attractive features in containers. These include:

- *Acorus gramineus* 'Ogon': initially it has an upright habit, then is arching and more relaxed, with narrow, tapering green leaves with golden variegated bands along their lengths. Other variegated forms include 'Hakuro-nishiki', 'Variegatus' with leaves striped cream and yellow, and 'Yodo-no-yuki' with leaves variegated pale green.
- *Carex oshimensis* 'Evergold': it has an attractive arching nature, with leaves variegated green and yellow.
- *Festuca glauca*: this grass has a tufted habit, and there are varieties with colored leaves—including blue, blue-green, and silvery-blue—which are extremely popular.

Monarda didyma
Bee Balm (UK/USA)
Oswego Tea (UK/USA)
Height: 2–3 feet
Spread: 15–18 inches
Hardy herbaceous perennial with dense heads of scarlet flowers throughout summer. There are several varieties.

Osteospermum ecklonis var. prostratum
African Daisy (UK)
Height: 6–9 inches
Spread: 12–15 inches
Bushy perennial with masses of daisy-like, white flowers with mustard-yellow centers in mid- and late summer.

Pachysandra terminalis 'Variegata'
Variegated Japanese Spurge (USA)
Height: 8–10 inches
Spread: 12–15 inches
Hardy, sub-shrubby plant with green leaves edged in white. It is ideal for smothering compost in a large tub.

Phormium tenax
New Zealand Flax (UK/USA)
New Zealand Hemp (UK/USA)
Height: 5–8 feet
Spread: 4–5 feet
Perennial, hardy in all but the coldest positions, with mid- to deep-green leaves (several colored forms).

Polygonum affine 'Dimity'
Knotweed (UK/USA)

Height: 6–8 inches

Spread: 12 inches

Hardy herbaceous perennial with spoon-shaped green leaves and deep-pink flowers throughout summer and into autumn.

Pulmonaria officinalis
Blue Lungwort (USA)

Jerusalem Sage (UK/USA)

Height: 12 inches

Spread: 12 inches

Hardy herbaceous perennial with white-spotted green leaves. Purple-blue flowers in late spring and early summer.

OTHER STACHYS TO TRY ...

Although *Stachys byzantina* is not fully hardy in all areas, where it is sheltered from cold and excessive wet weather it creates interest throughout the year. There are several attractive forms to consider growing, including:

- 'Cotton Boll' (also known as 'Sheila Macqueen'): it has large, felted, gray-green leaves and silvery flowers.
- 'Primrose Heron': this is a superb plant for year-round interest. During the summer, the leaves create a glorious golden carpet.
- 'Silver Carpet': this is an excellent plant with silky, silver leaves. It does not develop any flowers.

Sedum 'Autumn Joy'
Ice Plant (UK/USA)

Height: 18–24 inches

Spread: 18–20 inches

Hardy herbaceous perennial with fleshy leaves and heads of salmon-pink flowers that change to orange-brown in autumn.

Sempervivum tectorum
Common Houseleek (UK/USA)

Height: 2–3 inches

Spread: 6–12 inches

Hardy, rosette-forming evergreen succulent with mid-green leaves with maroon tips. Rose-purple flowers are produced in mid-summer.

Stachys byzantina
Lamb's Tongue (UK)

Lamb's Ears (UK/USA)

Height: 12–18 inches

Spread: 12–15 inches

Half-hardy perennial with foliage that persists throughout the year. Leaves have a silvery and woolly appearance.

Tiarella cordifolia
Foam Flower (UK/USA)

Height: 9–12 inches

Spread: 9–12 inches

Hardy, low-growing, evergreen perennial with maple-like mid-green leaves and spires of creamy-white flowers.

Tolmiea menziesii
Piggy-back Plant (UK/USA)

Youth-on-Age (UK/USA)

Height: 6–8 inches

Spread: 12–15 inches

Hardy evergreen with maple-like green leaves and spires of flowers on stems up to 2 feet high in early summer.

OTHER PHORMIUMS TO CONSIDER ...

Many Phormiums have colorful leaves that create spectacular features when in large containers on a patio or terrace. In areas where the temperature falls radically in winter, protect plants from severe frost. Incidentally, the all-green type is hardier than the variegated forms. Here are two forms of *Phormium tenax* to consider:

- 'Purpureum': this has superb, bronze-purple leaves.
- 'Variegatum': the leaves are striped green and yellow.

Additionally, there are some excellent forms of *Phormium cookianum* (also known as *Phormium colensoi*).

Flowering shrubs

How do I grow these plants?

Shrubs have a perennial, woody nature, and although some are quite short-lived, most will thrive in tubs until they outgrow their containers and have to be planted out in a garden. Select tubs or large pots for shrubs, using rustic tubs for those with an informal appearance. Large pots are more clinical in appearance and are ideal for shrubs with a formal and well-defined outline. Good drainage is essential, and you should always use soil-based compost.

POSITIONING FLOWERING SHRUBS

Unlike those shrubs that have attractive evergreen foliage, flowering types do not create interest throughout the year. Therefore, it is best not to use them as year-round focal points. Instead, position them in clusters with other shrubs, but without intruding on their outlines. Most flowering shrubs prefer a sunny position, but Camellias require a situation that is out of direct and early-morning sunlight. Watering is essential throughout the summer, and especially when shrubs are flowering. Make sure, however, that the compost does not become waterlogged by winter rains.

ROSES IN TUBS AND POTS

Planting Roses in tubs and pots is an exciting way to grow them on patios and terraces—or in small gardens. They are deciduous shrubs—choose either Miniature or Patio Roses.

Miniature Roses are best planted in large pots and where a compost depth of at least 9 inches is possible. Patio Roses are slightly larger and are better in tubs, where a compost depth of 12 inches is possible. Use soil-based compost for each of them.

Suitable Miniature Roses:
- 'Baby Austin': soft, peachy blooms are borne on this tiny miniature Rose.
- 'Cinderella': this has small, creamy white flowers with a spicy scent.
- 'Rainbow Starlight': this tiny plant produces little white blooms with yellow centers.
- 'Tom Thumb': this favorite miniature produces rich red, almost purple, flowers with superb foliage.

Suitable Patio Roses:
- 'Avandel': clusters of beautiful peach and yellow blooms with a light fragrance.
- 'Cal Poly': bright yellow flowers that grow well in patio pots.
- 'Doris Bennett': beautiful clusters of pink flowers with unusual pointed petals.
- 'Red Alert': scarlet flowers with lasting color, perfect for growing in pots on the patio.

Azaleas (Japanese) – evergreen types
Height: 1½–2 feet
Spread: 2–2½ feet
Small-leaved, bushy plants with masses of funnel-shaped flowers in spring. Colors include scarlet, pink, and white.
Use a slightly acid, loam-based compost.

Camellia x williamsii
Height: 15–6 feet
Spread: 4–5 feet
Also known as C. japonica x C. saluenensis. Evergreen, in colors from white and pale-pink to rose-purple. Flowering mainly in late winter and spring.

Choisya ternata
Mexican Orange Flower (UK/USA)
Height: 5–6 feet
Spread: 5–7 feet
Slightly tender evergreen shrub with scented, orange-blossom-like flowers mainly during mid- and late summer.

INEXPENSIVE ROSEMARY

Planting a large tub with three Rosemary plants can be expensive. Therefore, economize and take cuttings.
Step by step to success:
- In mid-summer, take 3–4 inch long cuttings and insert them in pots containing equal parts of moist peat and sharp sand.
- Place them outdoors in a cold frame or unheated greenhouse.
- When rooted, transfer them to 3 inch wide pots and overwinter them in a cold frame.
- Plant into a tub in spring. For a display that quickly fills a tub, plant five or seven cuttings in it.

Doronicum hirsutum (syn. Lotus hirsutus)

Height: 12–15 inches in a container
Spread: 15–18 inches in a container
Hardy, semi-herbaceous, woody-based shrub with heads of white, pink-flushed flowers in late summer and autumn.

Genista pilosa 'Vancouver Gold'

Broom (UK/USA)
Height: 6–12 inches
Spread: 3–4 feet
Compact, evergreen shrub with masses of deep golden-yellow flowers during late spring and early summer.

Hebe 'Margret'

Shrubby Veronica (UK)
Height: 12–15 inches
Spread: 1½–2 feet
Dwarf, compact, evergreen shrub that produces sky-blue flowers in late spring and early summer. It often also flowers in late summer.

Hydrangea macrophylla

Common Hydrangea (UK)
French Hydrangea (USA)
Height: 3–4 feet in a tub
Spread: 4–5 feet in a tub
Hardy deciduous shrub: use Hortensia types, with flowerheads 5–8 inches wide in mid-summer to early autumn.

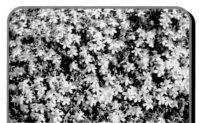

Hypericum olympicum

Olympic St-John's-Wort (USA)
Height: 8–12 inches
Spread: 12–15 inches
Hardy, low-growing evergreen shrub with golden-yellow flowers, about 1½ inches wide, in mid-summer.

Magnolia stellata

Star Magnolia (UK/USA)
Height: 15–6 feet in a tub
Spread: 5–6 feet in a tub
Hardy, slow-growing deciduous shrub with fragrant, white, large, star-like flowers during early and mid-spring.

Rosmarinus officinalis

Rosemary (UK/USA)
Height: 2–2½ feet in a tub
Spread: 2–2½ feet in a tub
Hardy, evergreen shrub with aromatic leaves and mauve flowers during spring, and intermittently later.

OTHER FLOWERING SHRUBS TO CONSIDER ...

- *Erica carnea*: a low-growing but bushy, evergreen shrub with flowers in many colors from late autumn to late spring.
- *Fuchsia magellanica*: a slightly tender shrub with crimson and purple, pendent flowers from mid-summer to autumn.
- *Hypericum* x *moserianum*: an evergreen shrub with a spreading nature and rich-yellow flowers from mid-summer to autumn. There is also the form 'Tricolor' which has attractively variegated leaves.
- *Lavandula angustifolia* 'Hidcote': a hardy, evergreen shrub with narrow, silvery-gray leaves and deep purple-blue flowers from mid- to late summer.
- *Mahonia* 'Charity': eventually a tall, evergreen shrub with arching spires of fragrant, deep yellow flowers from late autumn to late winter. Position it in a wind-sheltered corner, in full sun or dappled light.
- *Prunus incisa* 'Kojo Nomal': a small, flowering, ornamental cherry with red-centered pink flowers in spring.
- *Rhododendron yakushimanum*: a small, evergreen shrub with dark green leaves that produces masses of pink flowers, which later fade to white, during late spring and early summer.

Foliage shrubs

How do I grow foliage shrubs?

Tubs and large pots are essential when growing shrubs in containers. Some of these shrubs are evergreen and create attractive features throughout the year, while a few are deciduous. Some shrubs, as well as being deciduous and creating a fresh array of foliage each year, have leaves that assume rich colors in autumn before falling. Deciduous foliage shrubs tend to be slightly hardier than evergreen types, and therefore can be positioned in cooler places.

FOLIAGE SHRUBS FOR MEDITERRANEAN-STYLE GARDENS

Several of the foliage shrubs described on these pages will recall memories of vacations in warm climates, such as in Mediterranean countries. Yuccas and Cordylines create the impression of clinical warmth, while *Trachycarpus fortunei* (Chinese Windmill Palm) is a more dominant and distinctive plant. *Fatsia japonica* (False Castor Oil Plant) is another scene-setting plant for warm areas, and with the bonus of attractive foliage and distinctive white flowers in the autumn. Do not confuse this plant with *Ricinus communis* (Castor Oil Plant), which is best avoided.

COLORFUL SAGES ...

Several forms of the popular culinary Sage *Salvia officinalis* are ideal in containers. It is a short-lived, slightly tender shrubby plant that after a few years needs replacement when it becomes straggly. There are three superb forms with colored leaves; they grow about 1½–2 feet high and with a 15–18 inches spread—sometimes more:
- 'Icterina': superb green-and-gold leaves. It creates a dominant display.
- 'Purpurescens': stems and leaves suffused purple when young.
- 'Tricolor': gray-green leaves splashed creamy-white and suffused with pink and purple.

Acer palmatum 'Dissectum Atropurpureum'
Height: 3–4 feet in a tub
Spread: 4–5 feet in a tub
Hardy deciduous shrub with finely dissected bronze-red leaves. A closely related form has all-green leaves.

Aucuba japonica 'Variegata'
Gold Dust Plant (USA)
Spotted Laurel (USA)
Height: 3½–4½ feet in a tub
Spread: 3–4 feet in a tub
Hardy, bushy, evergreen shrub with a dome-like outline and dark green leaves peppered and splashed with yellow.

Choisya ternata 'Sundance'
Yellow-leaved Mexican Orange Blossom (UK/USA)
Height: 2½–3½ feet in a tub
Spread: 2½–3 feet in a tub
Slightly tender evergreen shrub with golden-yellow leaves all year round.

Elaeagnus pungens 'Maculata'
Variegated Thorny Elaeagnus (USA)
Height: 5–6 feet in a tub
Spread: 5–6 feet in a tub
Hardy, evergreen shrub with leathery, glossy-green leaves splashed with gold. Superb for winter color.

Euonymus fortunei 'Emerald 'n' Gold'
Height: 12–18 inches
Spread: 18–24 inches
Hardy evergreen shrub, densely covered with golden leaves that turn bronzy-pink in winter. Many other varieties.

Fatsia japonica
False Castor Oil Plant (UK)
Glossy-leaved Paper Plant (USA)
Height: 5–7 feet
Spread: 5–6 feet
Slightly tender evergreen shrub with large, glossy, hand-like green leaves, and white flowers in autumn.

Hebe x andersonii 'Variegata'
Shrubby Veronica (UK/USA)
Height: 2½–3 feet
Spread: 2–3 feet
Slightly tender evergreen shrub with cream and green leaves. Lavender flowers from mid-summer to autumn.

Hebe x franciscana
Shrubby Veronica (UK/USA)
Height: 12–18 inches
Spread: 12–18 inches
Slightly tender evergreen shrub with a dome-shaped outline and glossy-green leaves edged cream. Mauve-blue flowers.

Lonicera nitida 'Baggeson's Gold'
Yellow-leaved Chinese Honeysuckle (UK/USA)
Height: 3–5 feet in a tub
Spread: 2½–3 feet in a tub
Hardy evergreen shrub with small, golden leaves. It can be clipped.

Trachycarpus fortunei
Chinese Windmill Palm (UK/USA)
Chusan Palm (UK)
Height: 6–7 feet in a tub
Spread: 5–6 feet in a tub
Slightly tender, evergreen, slow-growing palm with large fans of glossy, mid-green leaves borne on long stalks.

Yucca filamentosa 'Variegata'
Variegated Adam's Needle (UK/USA)
Height: 2–2½ feet
Spread: 3–4 feet
Slightly tender evergreen shrub with rosettes of deep green leaves handsomely edged in whitish-yellow.

OTHER FOLIAGE SHRUBS TO CONSIDER ...

- *Berberis thunbergii* 'Aurea': superb hardy deciduous shrub with masses of bright, soft yellow leaves. There are several other colorfully leaved varieties, including 'Atropurpurea' (rich purple-red) and 'Atropurpurea 'Nana' (a dwarf form with rich purple-red leaves).
- *Calluna vulgaris*: hardy evergreen shrub with a low-growing habit. There are many attractively foliaged varieties, including 'Beoley Gold' (golden-yellow), 'Blazeaway' (foliage changes from gold through orange to red), 'Gold Haze' (bright gold) and 'Golden Carpet' (golden foliage flecked with orange and red during winter).
- *Cordyline australis* 'Purpurea': often known as a Cabbage Tree, it is slow-growing and has narrow, purple leaves. There are varieties in other colors.
- *Eucalyptus gunnii*: known as the Cider Gum and relatively hardy in temperate regions, this evergreen tree has a shrubby habit. It needs to be radically pruned in mid- to late spring to encourage the development of its distinctive juvenile foliage, which is round and blue-green. It needs a wind-sheltered position in full sun.
- *Hebe pinquifolia* 'Pagei': a low, evergreen shrub with small, grey leaves. During early summer, it has the bonus of bearing small, white flowers.
- *Ligustrum ovalifolium* 'Aureum': this is the Golden-leaved Privet, with rich golden-yellow leaves with green centers that certainly bring brightness to a patio.
- *Nandina domestica*: this is commonly known as the Chinese Sacred Bamboo, although it is not a bamboo. It has a slightly tender nature but grows well in containers on a sheltered patio. The leaf color changes from red, when the plant is young, to mid-green.
- *Sambucus racemosa* 'Sutherland Gold': eventually a large, deciduous shrub, but when young is ideal in a large tub. It has finely cut, golden-yellow leaves.

Dwarf and slow-growing conifers

Miniature and slow-growing conifers are well suited for growing in tubs and pots, as well as old stone sinks and firm-based troughs. They can also be planted in window boxes as part of a winter display. Well-drained, loam-based compost is essential, as well as good drainage. Once established, conifers are easy to grow and need little attention, although eventually most of them become too large for the container and are planted in the garden.

POSITIONING CONIFERS IN CONTAINERS

One of the main dangers to conifers when grown in containers, especially if planted in relatively small pots as compared with tubs, is that tall types are at risk from being blown over by gusting winds. Therefore, position them in the shelter of a wall. An additional safeguard is to plant wind-susceptible conifers in large or heavy-based containers, such as those formed of reconstituted stone. Also, use loam-based compost rather than a peat-based type. Other dangers are the compost becoming dry during summer, and excessively wet in winter when there is little chance of it drying.

Chamaecyparis lawsoniana 'Ellwoodii'
Slow-growing and ideal when small for planting in a container. It has short, feathery sprays of gray-green foliage that, in winter, assume shades of steel-blue. The form 'Ellwood's Golden Pillar' has golden-yellow foliage.

Chamaecyparis pisifera 'Boulevard'
Slow-growing, with a dense, narrowly conical outline packed with steel-blue foliage. The foliage is feathery and it is usually at its brightest when positioned in light shade. Plant it in a tub.

Chamaecyparis pisifera 'Filifera Aurea'
Slow-growing and very distinctive conifer, with a conical outline and spreading branches bearing drooping branchlets of thread-like, golden-yellow foliage. Eventually it forms a mop-headed plant. Plant it in a tub.

Juniperus chinensis 'Pyramidalis'
Slow-growing conifer with a conical outline and dense nature with dull, dark green leaves. The younger leaves have a bluish tinge and this creates an attractive feature when sunlight glances off them. Plant it in a tub.

Juniperus communis 'Depressa Aurea'
Slow-growing, with a spreading nature and packed with beautiful foliage, golden-yellow when young. With its spreading and, eventually, slightly mop-headed outline, it is best planted in a tub.

Juniperus communis 'Hibernica'
Slow-growing, with a columnar outline but, eventually, more narrowly oval. It is packed with needle-like, silver-backed leaves. When small it is ideal for window boxes, then large tubs and, eventually, the garden.

Juniperus scopularium 'Skyrocket'
Also known as *Juniperus virginiana* 'Skyrocket', it has a slow-growing, narrow habit and upright branches bearing silvery, blue-gray foliage. It has a distinctive outline and is best planted in a tub.

Juniperus squamata 'Blue Star'
Slow-growing, low conifer densely packed with silvery-blue foliage. It has a squat nature, but with shoots that attractively break the regularity of its outline. Plant it in a tub.

Juniperus squamata 'Meyeri'
A vigorous, semi-erect conifer which when young and before it becomes too large is ideal for growing in a tub. It is densely packed with glaucous-blue leaves and is ideal for creating a dominant blue feature on a patio.

Pinus sylvestris 'Beuvronensis'
Distinctive, miniature Scots Pine that creates a low, broad, cone-like outline of gray-green foliage. It is especially attractive in spring when new growth appears and is ideal for planting in a tub.

Taxus baccata 'Standishii'
Slow-growing, densely columnar conifer packed with golden-yellow leaves. It is ideal for creating a shape contrast on a patio and although at first it can be planted in a large pot, eventually it needs a tub to provide stability.

Thuja orientalis 'Aurea Nana'
Also known as *Platycladus orientalis* 'Aurea Nana', it is slow-growing with a neat, rounded habit. Ideal for planting first in a large pot, later transferring it to a tub. It reveals beautiful light yellow-green foliage and is especially attractive when positioned in full sun.

Thuja plicata 'Stoneham Gold'
Slow-growing, with a conical outline and bright golden foliage with coppery-bronze tips. Initially, plant it in a large pot, but later transfer to a tub.

OTHER CONIFERS TO CONSIDER ...

- *Abies balsamea* 'Hudsonia': dense and compact, with closely arranged short leaves that emit the fragrance of balsam.
- *Abies lasiocarpa* var. *arizonica* 'Compacta': slow-growing with a dense, conical outline. Attractive blue-gray foliage.
- *Chamaecyparis lawsoniana* 'Aurea Densa': slow-growing and compact with densely packed, golden-yellow foliage in short, flattened sprays.
- *Chamaecyparis lawsoniana* 'Minima Aurea': dwarf and slow-growing, with a conical outline and sprays of soft, golden-yellow foliage.
- *Juniperus communis* 'Compressa': slow-growing, with a columnar habit and narrow, prickly, silver-backed leaves. It is ideal for planting in window boxes, as well as in pots and troughs.
- *Juniperus horizontalis* 'Wiltonii': slow-growing, with long branches packed with glaucous-blue foliage. Plant it in a tub.
- *Juniperus* x *pfitzeriana* 'Old Gold': also known as *Juniperus* x *media* 'Old Gold', it has a compact habit and bronze-gold foliage.
- *Thuja occidentalis* 'Rheingold': slow-growing, with a conical outline and rich, old-gold foliage with a hint of amber.

Bamboos

Are bamboos suitable for containers?

Many bamboos grow remarkably well in containers that can be positioned on a patio, terrace, or around a house. They create color and interest throughout the year. Some have variegated leaves, while others are totally green. Some have colored canes. Several tall bamboos with small leaves produce an attractive rustling sound when blown by even the slightest breeze, and this introduces a relaxing and soothing quality to gardens.

CONTAINERS AND COMPOST FOR BAMBOOS

Large pots, wooden tubs, and square boxes create ideal homes for bamboos. Large, ornate, wide-based pots are ideal for low-growing bamboos, especially when positioned in an exotic garden. Large tubs and square boxes are better suited for tall-growing bamboos and are usually left in the same position until the compost is congested with roots. Garden soil often contains pests. Therefore, it is always best to use a combination of equal parts moisture-retentive peat-based compost and loam-based potting compost. Thoroughly mix them together before planting a bamboo.

BAMBOO CARE ...

- Stand the container out of direct sunlight and away from strong gusts of wind that dry the plants.
- Keep the compost moist—it may need watering several times a day during summer, especially if the weather is particularly hot.
- Brush snow from the leaves and canes before it freezes and becomes difficult to remove.
- If winters are especially severe, remember to wrap the container in sacking to prevent the compost freezing and damaging the roots.
- Repot any congested plants in spring. If necessary, plants can also be divided at the same time.

BAMBOOS FOR CONTAINERS

Low displays:
- *Pleioblastus pygmaeus*
- *Pleioblastus variegatus*
- *Pleioblastus viridistriatus*

Medium displays:
- *Fargesia murieliae*
- *Phyllostachys nigra*
- *Thamnocalamus tesselatus*

Tall and dominant displays:
- *Fargesia nitida*
- *Phyllostachys aurea*
- *Pseudosasa japonica*
- *Semiarundinaria fastuosa*
- *Thamnocalamus spathiflorus*

Fargesia nitida
Fountain Bamboo (UK/USA)
Queen of the Arundinarias (UK/USA)
Height: 12–15 feet
Spread: Clump-forming and non-invasive
Also known as *Arundinaria nitida* and *Sinarundinaria nitida*, it has bright green leaves and light purple canes.

Phyllostachys nigra
Black-stemmed Bamboo (UK/USA)
Black Bamboo (UK/USA)
Height: 8–10 feet
Spread: Moderately invasive
Also known as *Sinarundinaria nigra*, it has dark green leaves and canes at first green but later jet-black.

Pleioblastus viridistriatus
Golden-haired Bamboo (UK/USA)
Height: 3–4 feet
Spread: Moderately invasive
Also known as *Arundinaria viridistriatus*, it has purple-green canes and golden-yellow leaves with pea-green stripes.

Pseudosasa japonica
Arrow Bamboo (UK/USA)
Metake (UK/USA)
Height: 8–15 feet
Spread: Moderately invasive
Also known as *Arundinaria japonica*, it has sharply pointed, lance-shaped, dark glossy-green leaves.

Bonsai for patios

Bonsai is the ancient art of growing a tree in a shallow container and —by pruning leaves, shoots, roots, and branches—encouraging it to remain small and healthy. These trees can be either deciduous (meaning they lose their leaves in winter) or evergreen. Some are grown for their attractive foliage, and others for their flowers or berries. They are outdoor plants and can be displayed on supports or staging on a patio throughout the year.

What is bonsai?

DISPLAYING OUTDOOR BONSAI

Bonsai are best viewed at about waist height, cascading ones perhaps slightly higher. Permanent staging—freestanding or attached to a wall—is one way to display plants, but it should not be in continual shade. Other ways are to use tall display stands on which cascading bonsai can be placed, or "monkey poles," which are small platforms at the tops of stout wooden or concrete supports. Wherever your bonsai plants are positioned, make certain that slugs and snails cannot reach them, but that you will have all-weather access to the plants right throughout the year.

DO BONSAI NEED REGULAR ATTENTION?

Bonsai need attention throughout the year, but especially during their growing period.
- Watering: regular watering is needed during spring, summer, and into autumn. During winter, outdoor bonsai usually gain sufficient moisture from rain and, perhaps, snow. At the peak of summer, plants need to be watered several times a day. Let the water drain freely through the compost.
- Feeding: like all other plants, bonsai need to be fed regularly, although after being repotted wait until they are displaying active growth before applying fertilizers. From spring to early autumn apply a weak, general fertilizer. Use a proprietary bonsai fertilizer, and follow the directions.

BONSAI FOR PATIOS

Deciduous trees:
- *Acer buergerianum*
- *Acer palmatum*
- *Fagus sylvatica*
- *Ulmus procera*
- *Zelkova serrata*

Flowering shrubs, trees and climbers:
- *Forsythia*
- *Malus baccata*
- *Wisteria floribunda*

Conifers:
- *Ginkgo biloba* (deciduous)
- *Pinus sylvestris* (evergreen)
- *Tsuga heterophylla* (evergreen)

Acer palmatum
Japanese Maple (UK/USA)
An elegant, graceful tree with five-lobed (occasionally seven) leaves, which are green at first but by autumn reveal purplish or bronze hues. It can be used in most bonsai styles and is especially attractive as a specimen or in a group.

Pinus parviflora
Japanese White Pine (UK/USA)
Also known as *Pinus pentaphylla*, this evergreen conifer develops a low crown and wide-spreading branches. The purple bark is attractive, with patches of black scales. The blue-white needles are borne in groups of five.

Salix babylonica
Weeping Willow (UK/USA)
Vigorous, fast-growing, graceful tree, initially with an upward nature and later revealing pendent branches bearing slender, narrow, lance-shaped, pale to mid-green leaves. It also displays greenish-yellow catkins.

Wisteria floribunda
Japanese Wisteria (UK/USA)
Well-known deciduous climber with slender branches and leaves each formed of 12–19 oval leaflets. The spectacular, violet-blue, fragrant flowers are borne during late spring and early summer. There is a white-flowered form.

Bulbous plants

How do I grow these plants?

Bulbs and corms are nature's powerhouses of reserved energy, and the range of them for growing in tubs, pots, window boxes, troughs, and wall-baskets is wide. They include diminutive types, such as Crocuses and miniature Daffodils, and Lilies in pots that flood patios with color and fragrance. For success, it is essential that healthy bulbs are used. Inferior bulbs will never create the spectacular displays that are essential for containers on a patio.

GROWING LILIES IN POTS

The range of Lilies for growing in pots is extensive. They can be planted at any time between mid-autumn and early spring. Basal-rooting types do best, however, when planted in autumn. Here is the way to plant them.

- As soon as the bulbs are available, plant them singly in 6–8-inch wide pots. Use only a well-drained, soil-based compost.
- Place drainage material in the pot's base. Stem-rooting types are planted low down in the pot. A general clue is to plant all bulbs to about two and a half times their depth. *Lilium candidum*, however, should be planted with its nose just below the compost's surface.
- Water the compost and place the pots in a cool position: either plunge outdoors and cover with sharp sand, or place in a cool cellar or dark shed.
- When growth appears, gradually move the pots into better light and water to keep the compost evenly moist.

Lilies for growing in pots:
- *Lilium auratum* (Golden-rayed Lily): large, brilliant-white, bowl-shaped flowers during late summer and early autumn. Stem-rooting type.
- *Lilium candidum* (Madonna Lily): white, trumpet-shaped flowers with a honey-like fragrance and golden anthers in early and mid-summer. Basal-rooting type.
- *Lilium hansonii*: pale orange-yellow, fragrant, Turk's-cap shaped flowers with brown spots during early and mid-summer. Stem-rooting type.
- *Lilium longiflorum* (Easter Lily): white, trumpet-shaped flowers with golden pollen during mid- and late summer. Stem-rooting type.
- *Lilium speciosum*: fragrant, bowl-shaped, white flowers shaded crimson during late summer and into early autumn. A warm patio is essential; alternatively, grow it in a cool greenhouse. Stem-rooting type.

GETTING A BETTER DISPLAY FROM DAFFODILS

Plant Daffodil bulbs in early autumn for a feast of glorious and radiant color in spring.
- Clean and stand a tub in position. Form a 2-inch thick layer of coarse drainage material in the base.
- Add and firm good-quality, loam-based compost to within 8 inches of the tub's top.

- Space healthy, good-quality Daffodil bulbs about 3 inches apart. Trickle and firm compost between them.
- Position a further layer of bulbs, with their bases between the ones already in position.
- Add and firm compost to within 1 inch of the tub's rim. Gently but thoroughly water the compost.

Chionodoxa gigantea
Glory of the Snow (UK/USA)
Height: 8 inches
Spread: 3–4 inches
Pale violet-blue flowers, about 1½ inches across, from late winter to mid-spring. Each flower has a white center.

Crocus chrysanthus hybrids
Crocus (UK/USA)
Height: 3–4 inches
Spread: 2–3 inches
Well-known cormous plants that produce cup-shaped, honey-scented flowers in many colors during late winter and early spring.

Galanthus nivalis
Common Snowdrop (UK/USA)
Height: 3–7 inches
Spread: 3–5 inches
Distinctive, with strap-like leaves and white flowers from mid-winter to early spring. 'Flore-plena' has double flowers.

Hyacinthus orientalis
Common Hyacinth (UK/USA)
Garden Hyacinth (UK/USA)
Height: 16–9 inches
Spread: 4–6 inches
Flower spires packed with flowers in a wide color range, including white, yellow, pink, red, and blue, in spring.

Iris danfordiae
Miniature Iris (UK/USA)
Height: 4 inches
Spread: 3–4 inches
Honey-scented, lemon-yellow flowers, up to 3 inches wide, during mid- and late winter.

Muscari armeniacum
Grape Hyacinth (UK/USA)
Height: 8–10 inches
Spread: 3–4 inches
Clump-forming, with narrow, green leaves and upright stems bearing azure-blue flowers during mid- and late spring.

Narcissus bulbocodium
Hoop Petticoat Daffodil (UK/USA)
Height: 3–5 inches
Spread: 3 inches
Bulbous, with distinctive, yellow, 1 inch long, funnel-shaped flowers during late winter and early spring.

Narcissus – Trumpet types
Daffodil (UK/USA)
Height: 13–18 inches
Spread: 3–4 inches
Popular bulbous plants, with distinctive trumpet-like flowers in yellow or white outdoors during spring.

Tulipa greigii
Height: 9–12 inches
Spread: 5–6 inches
Hardy species Tulip that produces blunt-pointed, orange-scarlet flowers during mid-spring.

Tulips – Single Early
Height: 6–15 inches
Spread: 4–5 inches
Select short types for containers. Wide color range for flowers during mid-spring. Flowers often open flat. Double Early Tulips (illustrated above) can also be grown in containers; use short types to avoid wind damage.

BULB "FACTS OF LIFE"
- Always buy good-quality bulbs for planting in containers. Some large-flowered Daffodil bulbs are sold for naturalizing in grass, but these are not suitable for containers.
- Don't reuse in outdoor containers any bulbs that earlier were forced into early flower indoors. These bulbs are best naturalized around shrubs in borders.
- Don't mix different Lily bulbs when using large containers, such as tubs.
- Don't mix different varieties of Hyacinths in the same container, as they may not all flower at the same time and the dramatic nature of the display will be diminished.

OTHER BULBS TO CONSIDER ...
- *Anemone blanda* (Spring-flowering Windflower): blue flowers from late winter to mid-spring.
- *Chionodoxa luciliae* (Glory of the Snow): blue, white-centered flowers during late winter and early spring.
- *Eranthis hyemalis* (Winter Aconite): lemon-yellow flowers during late winter and early spring.
- *Ipheion uniflora*: white to deep blue flowers in spring.
- *Iris reticulata*: deep purple-blue, with orange blazes, during late winter and early spring.
- *Leucojum vernum* (Snowflake): white, in late winter and early spring.
- *Tulipa fosteriana*: scarlet, in mid-spring.

Culinary herbs for patios

How can I grow herbs on a patio?

There are many containers which can be used to grow herbs on patios, including growing-bags. Window boxes are ideal homes for small herbs (see below), while pots and planters are other solutions to having culinary herbs within easy reach of a kitchen. Unlike when grown in herb gardens in borders—where plants can be left undisturbed for several years—be prepared to check plants in containers regularly, and to remove invasive types.

HARVESTING AND STORING CULINARY HERBS

All herbs are better for being used fresh, but there are several months when picking is not possible for some plants.

- Herbs can be dried or frozen for winter use (as such, they will be unsuitable as a garnish). However, remember that the flavor of dried herbs becomes intensified, and you will need only half the quantity compared to fresh herbs.
- When freezing herbs, pick and put them in plastic bags and place in rigid containers to prevent them being squashed when in a freezer. The most suitable ones for freezing are Mint, Chives and Parsley.

GROWING HERBS IN WINDOW BOXES

Window boxes in summer are ideal homes for small herbs. In the cycle of using window boxes, one planted with herbs can be put in place immediately the spring-flowering display has been removed (see page 52 for details of using window boxes).

Although herbs can be planted directly into compost in a window box, it is usually better to leave them in individual pots and to position them directly in a window box; pack moist peat around them. Invasive herbs such as Mint are then kept under control. Additionally, herbs which cease to be attractive can be removed and young plants put in their place.

GROWING HERBS IN POTS

No patio is complete without a few pots of herbs near the kitchen door.

- Groups of ornamental pots, as well as more functional types, are ideal homes for herbs, from Chives and Mint to Parsley and Thyme.
- Most of these herbs can be left in pots and other containers for several years, but Parsley is usually grown as an annual and fresh plants will need to be raised each year.
- Bay trees are often grown as half-standards in tubs or large pots. Always use large containers and soil-based compost; this gives the plant a stable base.

Allium schoenoprasum
Chives
Height: 16–9 inches
Spread: 8–10 inches
Bulbous, hardy perennial with grass-like, tubular leaves with a mild onion-like flavor, and starry flowers.

Laurus nobilis
Bay
Height: 4–6 feet in a tub
Spread: 2–2½ feet in a tub
Hardy evergreen tree; ideal as a half-standard in a tub. The glossy, mid-green leaves are aromatic and added to food.

Melissa officinalis
Balm
Height: 1½–2 feet in a tub
Spread: 12–18 inches in a tub
Herbaceous perennial, ideal for a tub. The leaves have a refreshing lemon scent and are ideal for flavoring drinks.

Mentha spicata
Mint—Common Mint or Spearmint
Height: 12–18 inches
Spread: Invasive
Herbaceous perennial with aromatic leaves which have a distinctive spearmint flavor; used in mint sauce.

Origanum majorana
Marjoram
Height: 1½–2 feet
Spread: 12–15 inches
Bushy, slightly tender perennial known as Sweet or Knotted Marjoram. Sweetly aromatic leaves.

Petroselinum crispum
Parsley
Height: 12–18 inches
Spread: 9–15 inches
Hardy biennial that is invariably grown as an annual, with branching stems bearing mid-green leaves; it is used to flavor and garnish.

Rosmarinus officinalis
Rosemary
Height: 3–4 feet in a tub
Spread: 1½–2½ feet in a tub
Hardy, evergreen shrub with aromatic leaves. Mauve, white, or bright blue flowers during late spring and summer.

Ruta graveolens
Rue
Height: 12–18 inches in a pot
Spread: 12–15 inches in a pot
Hardy, evergreen shrub with deeply divided, blue-green leaves. When picked and chopped they are added to salads.

Salvia officinalis
Sage
Height: 1–1½ feet in a tub
Spread: 1–1½ feet in a tub
Evergreen, slightly tender shrub with gray-green, wrinkled leaves that produces violet-blue flowers during early and mid-summer.

Thymus vulgaris
Thyme – Common Thyme
Height: 4–8 inches
Spread: 9–12 inches
Hardy, low-growing evergreen shrub with aromatic, dark green leaves that are added to flavor food and stuffings.

HERBS IN PLANTERS

Growing herbs in planters—containers with cupped holes around their sides—is ideal for collections of small herbs in a small area. The range of their shapes and colors will create both an attractive feature and a supply of culinary herbs throughout summer.

- Some planters are formed of plastic and others of glass-fiber and reconstituted stone.
- Because plants are usually left in the planter for several years, ensure that excess water can easily escape from the planter's base, and that a loam-based compost is used.
- To keep invasive herbs small, regularly nip off their growing tips.

AROMATIC THYMES

In addition to the Common Thyme (*Thymus vulgaris*) with its aromatic leaves, others have attention-seeking bouquets. Here are two of them:

- Caraway-scented Thyme (*Thymus herba-barona*): sometimes known as the Seed-cake Thyme, it has caraway-scented, mat-green leaves borne on plants with a prostrate nature. Tubular, pale-lilac flowers appear in terminal clusters in early summer.
- Lemon-scented Thyme (*Thymus x citriodorus*): with an appearance similar to Common Thyme, it has lemon-scented leaves. For extra color, try the colored or variegated-leaved forms. It is used in the same way as Common Thyme.

AROMATIC MINTS

- Apple Mint (*Mentha rotundifolia* or *Mentha suaveolens*): sometimes known as the Round Leaf Mint, it has pale green leaves that emit the fragrance of apples.
- Brandy Mint (*Mentha x piperita*): spear-like to heart-shaped green leaves that are often tinged reddish-purple and that have a strong peppermint redolence.
- Ginger Mint (*Mentha x gracilis*; also known as *Mentha x gentilis*): mid-green leaves that have the redolence of ginger.
- Peppermint Mint (*Mentha requienii*): also known as the Corsican Mint and Crème de Menthe Mint, it has pale green leaves with a peppermint scent.

Climbing plants

Can climbers be grown in containers?

It is possible to grow a wide range of climbers in containers and to create magnificent displays. These plants include perennial climbers, annual climbers, and herbaceous types. Some of these, such as Clematis and Wisteria, are famed for their flowers, and others for their colorful foliage. Many are also superbly fragrant. However, when climbers are grown in containers they need regular attention to ensure that the compost is evenly moist throughout summer.

SUITABLE CONTAINERS FOR CLIMBERS

For climbers that remain in the same container for several years, it is essential that the container holds as much compost as possible. The larger the amount of compost, the less the roots are at risk from overheating during summer and freezing in winter. Additionally, wooden containers, with their ability to thermally insulate compost, are better than metal types which heat up quickly in summer and remain cold in winter. Large earthenware pots are ideal for climbers. If the container is large, always put it in position before filling it with compost, or you may not be able to move it.

CREATING TRIPOD DISPLAYS

Instead of creating a screen-like display of flowers and leaves against a trellis, try a tripod display. This is ideal for producing a display that can be viewed from all sides. Suitable climbers for this include half-hardy annuals and the herbaceous *Humulus lupulus* 'Aureus' (Yellow-leaved Hop).
- Use a large tub and insert 4–5 5–6-foot long bamboo canes into compost at the edge of a tub.
- Angle their tops toward the center and tie them together, about 6 inches from the top.
- Use several plants if you want to create a quick display.

THREE STUNNING DISPLAYS TO TRY...

- Put three plants of the spectacular *Clematis macropetala* in the top of an old, upright, wooden barrel. Ensure the barrel is well drained and use soil-based compost. In late spring and early summer it will clothe the barrel with 2–3 inches wide, light and dark blue flowers.
- Position a tub or a large terra-cotta pot alongside ornate railings and plant a large-flowered Clematis in it. There are many to choose from, and it will drench the railings in color.
- Construct a wigwam of bamboo canes in a tub and plant several plants of the delightfully fragrant Sweet Pea in it to grow up the canes.

Cobaea scandens
Cathedral Bells (UK)
Cup-and-Saucer Vine (UK/USA)
Height: 6 feet in a container
Half-hardy perennial usually grown as a half-hardy annual. It produces purple-green flowers throughout summer.

Eccremocarpus scaber
Chilean Glory Flower (UK)
Glory Flower (USA)
Height: 6 feet in a container
Slightly tender (in temperate climates) evergreen climber. Tubular, orange-scarlet flowers are borne throughout summer.

Humulus lupulus 'Aureus'
Yellow European Hop (USA)
Yellow-leaved Hop (UK/USA)
Height: 5–6 feet – in a container
Hardy herbaceous perennial with scrambling stems bearing masses of five-lobed, bright yellowish-green leaves.

Ipomoea tricolor
Morning Glory (UK/USA)
Height: 5–6 feet in a container
Half-hardy annual with large, trumpet-shaped flowers in blue or purple during late summer and into autumn.

GROWING SWEET PEAS

Lathyrus odoratus (Sweet Pea) is a well-known climber, with masses of flowers in many colors throughout summer. Colors include shades of red, blue, pink, and purple, as well as white.

- The Sweet Pea is really a hardy annual, but to produce quick displays in containers it is invariably grown as a half-hardy annual.
- Seeds are sown in gentle warmth in a greenhouse early in the year, for planting into containers as soon as all risk of frost has passed.
- For growing in pots, always choose dwarf varieties of Sweet Pea.
- Regularly pick the flowers to encourage further ones to develop.

Lathyrus odoratus
Sweet Pea (UK/USA)
Height: 2–6 feet in a container
Hardy annual usually grown as a half-hardy annual. Wide range of scented flowers from early summer to autumn.

Passiflora caerulea
Blue Passion Flower (UK)
Common Passion Flower (UK)
Height: 6–8 feet in a container
Slightly tender scrambling deciduous climber with 3 inches wide, white flowers with blue centers from early to late summer.

Thunbergia alata
Black-eyed Susan (UK)
Clockvine (USA)
Height: 4–6 feet in a container
Hardy annual climber with orange-yellow, 2 inches wide flowers with dark centers produced from early summer through to autumn.

Tropaeolum majus
Garden Nasturtium (USA)
Nasturtium (UK)
Height: 5–6 feet in a container
Hardy annual (some climbing, others low and trailing) with flowers in many colors throughout summer.

Tropaeolum perigrinum
Canary Creeper (UK/USA)
Canary Bird Flower (USA)
Height: 5–6 feet in a container
Half-hardy perennial that is usually grown as a hardy annual. Irregularly shaped yellow flowers appear from mid-summer to autumn.

CLEMATIS FOR CONTAINERS

Clematis will create dramatic feasts of color, but can be difficult to grow in a container, usually because it is too small and does not hold sufficient compost to provide a reserve of moisture. If these problems can be overcome, however, the following are possible patio brighteners.

- *Clematis armandii*: evergreen climber with saucer-shaped, 2–2½-inch wide, white flowers in mid-spring, sometimes slightly later. The form 'Apple Blossom' has pink and white flowers, while 'Snowdrift' produces pure white flowers. It is vigorous and needs a large structure up which to climb.
- *Clematis florida* 'Sieboldii': usually deciduous, but in warm climates is semi-evergreen, with a shrubby and sparse habit. During mid- and late spring it bears white, double flowers.
- Clematis—large-flowered types: these are popular clematis but not always successful unless the compost remains cool and moist. Many superb varieties and colors. Rather than providing special supports, position the container near an ornamental wrought-iron fence.
- *Clematis macrocarpa*: during late spring and early summer it displays 2–3-inch wide, light and dark blue flowers. See far left for growing it in a large barrel.

GROWING WISTERIA IN A POT

Wisteria is a woody, deciduous climber that normally grows against a wall, where it produces pendulous clusters of fragrant, violet-blue flowers during late spring and early summer. Use *Wisteria floribunda* (Japanese Wisteria), which is not as vigorous as *Wisteria sinensis* (Chinese Wisteria). In addition to the regular blue-flowered type, there is a white form. It can also be grown in a tub or large terra-cotta pot on a wind-sheltered patio. Train a single stem upward to create a canopy at head height. Support the stem, as well as providing a framework of wires for the laterally trained branches. Both winter and summer pruning will be necessary to prevent excessive growth.

Plants for lobbies and porches

How do I grow these plants?

Lobbies and porches are halfway homes between outdoors and indoors, and provide good conditions for growing frost-tender indoor plants. Lobbies are enclosed areas, but porches tend to be more exposed to outdoor weather—especially those that are completely open in design, without any kind of outer door. Indoor hanging-baskets (with drip-trays to prevent water spilling on floors) enable a wide range of foliage and flowering plants to be grown in these areas.

PLANTING TECHNIQUES

There are two main ways of growing plants in indoor hanging-baskets. The first method involves removing their growing pots and planting a group of plants in compost, while the other way is to leave them in their pots and just to place them in a flat-based hanging-basket. The latter method enables plants to be easily swapped and those not looking attractive to be removed. The techniques of these methods are described and illustrated on page 57. Whichever method is chosen, ensure that the compost is evenly moist, especially during summer. In winter, it can be kept slightly drier.

FERNS FOR LOBBIES AND PORCHES

In addition to "proper" ferns, there are others that have a similar appearance and often have the word "fern" in their common name. Here is a selection of ferns and their "lookalikes."

- *Asparagus densiflorus* 'Myersii' (Foxtail Fern): upright, then arching, bottlebrush-like stems bearing mid-green leaves. Minimum winter temperature 45°F. Either plant it in a hanging-basket or position it in a wall bracket.
- *Asparagus densiflorus* 'Sprengeri' (Emerald Fern): arching, wiry stems bearing mid-green leaves. Minimum winter temperature 45°F. Plant in a hanging-basket or position in a wall bracket.
- *Asplenium bulbiferum* (Mother Fern): large, finely cut fronds with small bulbils that weigh them down. Minimum winter temperature 39°F. Plant in a hanging-basket or position in a wall bracket.
- *Nephrolepis exaltata* (Ladder Fern or Sword Fern): upright and cascading, deeply divided, sword-like fronds. 'Bostoniensis' has more arching fronds and 'Marshallii' develops pale green, densely crested fronds. Minimum winter temperature 45–50°F. Avoid drafts, and plant in a hanging-basket.
- *Pellaea rotundifolia* (Button Fern): unusual fern, with small, button-like, leathery fronds on wiry stems.

Begonia x tuberhybrida 'Pendula'
Trailing Tuberous-rooted Begonia (UK/USA)
Height: 6–8 inches
Trailing: 12–15 inches
Tender, tuberous-rooted plant with rose-like summer flowers in many colors.

Campanula isophylla 'Krystal' varieties
Italian Bellflower (USA)
Height: 6 inches
Trailing: to 18 inches
Hardy perennial with masses of star-shaped, blue or white flowers, 1 inch wide, from early to late summer.

Chlorophytum comosum 'Variegatum'
Spider Plant (UK/USA)
Height: 8–12 inches
Spread: 18–24 inches
Tender houseplant with long, narrow, variegated leaves and long stems that produce plantlets at their ends.

Chrysanthemum morifolium – Cascade Types
Cascade Chrysanthemum (UK/USA)
Height: 4–6 inches
Trailing: 12–18 inches or more
Frost-tender plants with a trailing nature and small, daisy-like flowers, each about 1 inch wide, in many colors.

LOBBY PLANTS FOR WALL BRACKETS

Some small, relatively hardy house-plants are ideal for positioning on their own in wall brackets—but avoid places where the temperature falls below 41°F. Here is a selection.

- *Callisia elegans* (Striped Inch Plant): fleshy, dull green leaves with white stripes and purple undersides.
- *Chlorophytum comosum* 'Variegatum': popular houseplant with long, narrow leaves that display white and green stripes. It produces plantlets at the ends of long stems.
- *Ficus radicans* 'Variegata' (Variegated Trailing Fig): cascading, wiry stems and lance-shaped, slender-pointed, mid-green leaves with creamy edges.
- *Oplismenus hirtellus* 'Variegatus' (Variegated Basket Vine): it creates a mass of tumbling stems bearing white-and-pink striped leaves.
- *Stenotaphrum secundatum* 'Variegatum' (Variegated Buffalo Grass): long, narrow, green leaves, up to 5 inches long, banded in white.
- *Tolmiea menziesii* (Piggy-back Plant, Mother of Thousands, or Youth-on-age): elliptic to oval leaves, about 2 inches long, striped in cream. There are several other forms, some of which are striped in silver.
- *Zebrina pendula* (Silvery Inch Plant): also known as *Tradescantia zebrina*, it has thick stems bearing mid-green leaves with two silvery bands on their upper surfaces.

Helichrysum petiolare
Licorice Plant (USA)
Height: 12–15 inches
Spread: 18–20 inches or more
Tender, shrubby perennial with lax, silvery-gray stems and leaves. There are several forms with variegated or colored leaves.

Pelargoniums – Continental Geraniums
Balcon and Cascade Geraniums
Height: 8–12 inches
Trailing and cascading
Frost-tender plants with masses of flowers throughout summer. Wide color range. Buy established plants.

Pelargonium peltatum
Trailing Geranium (USA)
Ivy-leaved Geranium (UK)
Height: 4–6 inches
Trailing: 18 inches or more
Tender perennial, with fleshy mid-green, ivy-shaped leaves. Carmine-pink flowers in summer. Several superb varieties.

MEDLEYS OF PLANTS FOR HANGING-BASKETS

Using several different plants in a hanging-basket creates long displays and with more varied interest.

- For a cool lobby: a central *Calceolaria* x *herbeohybrida* (Pouch Flower) with trailing Petunias and Lobelias creates a colorful display in summer. By using yellow and blue, the display is ideal for positioning in a white-walled porch or lobby.
- For a warm lobby: position a Dracaena in the center, with trailing ivy-leaved *Pelargonium* (Geraniums) and Lobelias around it. A variation is to use a *Begonia* x *tuberhybrida* instead of the Dracaena.
- For an all-green display: flowering plants are not essential to hanging-basket displays. Try a mixture of *Asparagus densiflorus* (Asparagus Fern) positioned in the center, surrounded by variegated small-leaved *Hedera helix* (Ivies), *Zebrina pendula* (Silvery Inch Plant; also known as *Tradescantia zebrina*) and *Sedum sieboldii* 'Medio-variegatum' (Variegated Siebold's Stonecrop). This arrangement is highlighted when positioned against a white wall.
- For a color-packed display: plant a pink-flowered *Begonia* 'Gloire de Lorraine' in the center, with trailing variegated small-leaved *Hedera helix* (Ivies), cascading Fuchsias, and trailing *Begonia* x *tuberhybrida* 'Pendula' (Tuberous Begonia).

Pericallis x hybrida
Florist's Cineraria (UK/USA)
Height: 12–15 inches
Spread: 10–15 inches
Half-hardy perennial, also known as *Senecio hybridus* and *Senecio cruentus*. Domed heads in many colors. Replace plants as necessary.

Saxifraga stolonifera 'Tricolor'
Strawberry Saxifrage (USA)
Height: 4–6 inches
Trailing: 12–18 inches, or more
Frost-tender plant with large, green leaves variegated pink and pale yellow. Use on its own or with other plants.

Growing vegetables in containers

Can I grow vegetables in containers?

Several vegetables can be grown in containers on a patio, and the most successful types are those cultivated for their leaves, pods, or fruits (tomatoes). A few root crops, such as radishes, are possible in tubs, growing-bags and window boxes, while carrots and beets can be put in deep boxes of friable compost. Large vegetables are best reserved for vegetable plots in a garden. Grow potatoes in growing-bags, deep pots, and tubs (see right).

SELECTING THE RIGHT CONTAINER

To gardeners with a large vegetable plot in a garden, food plants in containers on a patio are superfluous. Yet where balconies, courtyards, and patios are the only gardening areas the thought of fresh vegetables is magnetic in its appeal. It is essential to match the vegetable to a container, and suitable partnerships are suggested on these pages. Slugs and snails are the major pests, but this risk can be reduced by putting ground-level containers on bricks. Growing-bags can be placed on old, cut-down pallet bases sitting on four bricks. This also makes it easier to reposition the bags, if necessary.

TOMATOES IN HANGING-BASKETS

- Line a 18-inch wide wire-framed basket with black polyethylene.
- When all risk of frost has passed, plant 2–3 tomato plants in a basket. Partly fill the basket with loam-based compost; it produces shorter plants than peat-based types.
- Use a variety such as 'Golden Nugget', 'Small Fry,' or 'Sweet One-Hundred'. Firm compost around the plants and trim the polyethylene slightly above the basket's edge. Additionally, use a knife to slit holes in the base to enable water to drain away.
- Plants are naturally bushy and do not need to have sideshoots removed. Pick fruits as soon as they color.

VEGETABLES IN WINDOW BOXES

A wider range of vegetables can be grown in window boxes than in hanging-baskets:

- Cucumbers: buy young plants as soon as all risk of frost has passed and plant one in the center of the window box. Pinch out the growing point when the plant has 6–7 leaves. Shoots can be left to trail.
- Sweet peppers: when all risk of frost has passed, put 2–3 young plants in a window box.
- Tomatoes: put two bush-type tomato plants in a window box as soon as all risk of frost has passed. It is not necessary to remove sideshoots.

Eggplant
Also known as aubergines, these frost-tender plants can be grown outdoors on warm patios. Fertile compost is essential. Harvest the fruits when they have an even color and are still glossy.
Grow in: Growing-bags, large pots, wall-baskets, mangers.

Beans – bush type
These do not need supports and produce masses of bean pods on low-growing plants. Full sun and moisture-retentive compost are essential. Pick the beans while they are small and tender.
Grow in: growing-bags, large pots.

Zucchini
Also known as courgettes. These frost-tender plants can be grown outdoors on warm patios. Grow in fertile compost. Harvest the fruits when they are still young and small.
Grow in: growing-bags, wall-baskets, mangers.

Cucumbers
Compact, bush-like varieties are essential and can be harvested within two months of being planted. Position them 10–12 inches apart.
Grow in: growing-bags, window boxes, wall-baskets, mangers.

POTATOES IN TUBS

Tubs and large pots can be used to grow early potatoes.

- In early spring, thoroughly clean the container and check that there are drainage holes in its base. Place the container in position and raise it up on bricks.
- Form a 4–5-inch thick layer of loam-based compost in the base and place 4–5 seed potatoes on top.
- Cover them with 4–5 inches of compost. As shoots develop, cover them with further compost until within 1½ inches of the rim.
- Keep the compost moist but not waterlogged and harvest them about three months later.

Lettuces

Choose small varieties and in a growing-bag grow eight plants. Loose-leaf types are best and over a long period a few leaves can be removed at one time.

Grow in: growing-bags.

ADVANTAGES OF GROWING-BAGS

As well as being relatively inexpensive to buy, growing-bags have several other advantages:

- They are lightweight and therefore ideal for use on balconies, as well as on patios and terraces;
- The compost is clean and free from all pests and diseases;
- They are easily transported home and stored before use;
- Good growth is possible, provided that plants are fed regularly once they have become established;
- They have a variety of uses, ranging from vegetables to herbs. The bags can even be recycled for further use during the following year.

PREPARING A GROWING-BAG FOR USE

For success with a growing-bag, spend some time in its preparation.

- Clean the outside, then shake to loosen the compost; place it on a flat, level surface.
- If slugs and snails are likely to be a problem, place the bag on a board slightly raised above the ground.
- As indicated on the bag itself, cut windows in the bag. Sometimes there is a central band which prevents the sides splaying apart.
- Pierce a number of drainage holes, as indicated on the bag.
- Before putting plants into the bag, saturate the compost with water and let it drain.

Potatoes

Choose "first early" varieties and plant in mid-spring for a mid-summer crop. Alternatively, plant in mid-summer for an early-winter crop, but protection against frost is essential.

Grow in: tubs, large pots, special potato-growing containers, growing-bags.

Radishes

Treat these rapid-growing vegetables as a space filler in containers where vegetables are being grown. Sow seeds in a succession from mid-spring to mid-summer; harvest the radishes when they are still young.

Grow in: tubs, window boxes, growing-bags.

VEGETABLES IN GROWING-BAGS

The number of plants refer to a standard growing-bag.

- Bush green beans: plant six bushy plants. Pods are ready to be harvested when they snap when bent—about 4–6 inches long.
- Lettuces: grow eight lettuces in a bag.
- Tomatoes: plant 3–4 young plants. Supports are essential (proprietary types are available). Regularly water and feed plants.
- Zucchini: use two plants. Water and feed regularly and as soon as the fruits are young and tender, harvest them. This encourages the development of further zucchini.

Sweet peppers

Also known as capsicums, these tender vegetables need fertile compost and plenty of sun and water in order to thrive. Do not plant outdoors until all risk of frost has passed.

Grow in: growing-bags, wall-baskets, mangers, window boxes.

Tomatoes

Popular frost-tender plants—a warm, wind-sheltered position is essential. Use cordon types (single, upright stem) in pots, but remember that bush types are much easier to grow.

Grow in: cordon types—pots; bush types—hanging-baskets, wall-baskets, mangers.

Growing fruit in containers

Can I grow fruit in containers?

Several types of fruit can be grown in containers, but they are longer-lived than vegetables and therefore require more care and attention from one year to another. The majority of container-grown fruits need large containers, such as tubs and large pots. Strawberries, however, can be grown in hanging-baskets and planters, as well as in large barrels with planting holes cut in their sides, a traditional method dating back more than a hundred years.

ASPECT AND CARE

A warm, wind-sheltered position is essential, as well as regularly and thoroughly watering the compost throughout summer. Good drainage is vital, and always use loam-based compost rather than peat-based types. In winter, use polyethylene or two large tiles angled like a tent over the compost to prevent it becoming too wet; this causes root decay as well as putting the plants at risk from frozen compost. Birds soon damage buds and fruits if they are not prevented by the use of netting. A wire-netting cage is best, but this is an expensive way to protect your fruits.

STRAWBERRIES IN HANGING-BASKETS

Strawberries do not need a large amount of compost, and as well as being planted in hanging-baskets do well in other compost-restricted containers such as window boxes and wall-baskets.

• Use a seed-raised variety and buy young plants in late spring or early summer, when all risk of frost has passed. If there is a risk of frost after being planted, place a few sheets of newspaper over them.
• Put three plants in a large hanging-basket, or about 8 inches apart in window boxes and wall-baskets.

STRAWBERRIES IN PLANTERS

Some planters—with holes in their sides—are made of glass-fiber, others of reconstituted stone. Whatever the material, they create ideal homes for strawberry plants, which can be left in position for 2–3 years before replanting is needed.

• Check that drainage holes in the base are not blocked. Then, place 2 inches of coarse drainage material in the base.
• Roll a piece of wire-netting (slightly less in length than the depth of the planter) into a tube about 3 inches wide. Place it vertically in the planter's base and fill with large stones.
• Fill the planter with loam-based compost to level with the first planting hole.
• Put a strawberry plant in the hole, with its roots spread out on the compost, and add and firm further compost.
• Add more compost and, in stages, both plant the container and fill with compost.
• Put strawberry plants in the top. Lightly but thoroughly water the compost.
• Several varieties can be used, including 'Earligrow' (early and mid-summer fruiting), 'Red Chief' (mid-summer fruiting), and 'Sparkle' (fruiting in late summer and into autumn).

STRAWBERRIES IN BARRELS AND CASKS

Wooden barrels, with their traditional shape and rustic nature, have long been used to decoratively and productively grow strawberries. Large, waist-high barrels, earlier used to transport beer, can be modified and used to create eye-catching features on a patio. Converting a large barrel is described on page 71.

• Casks—usually about knee height— can also be modified, either with holes cut in their sides or just with one end taken out, the cask turned upright and strawberry plants inserted in the top.

• Whether strawberries are planted in barrels or casks, good drainage is essential to prevent their roots becoming damaged.

Apples
If there is only space for one "tree" fruit, choose an apple. The best way is to buy a "family" tree and to grow as a pyramid. Picking and eating times depend on the variety (as indicated on page 49).

Blueberries
These low-growing bush fruits are increasingly popular and easy to grow. Birds can be a problem when fruits start to ripen, but netting will keep them at bay. Using both ericaceous compost and soft water is essential.

APPLES IN TUBS AND LARGE POTS

Apples are a popular tree fruit to grow in a container, but there are a few vital considerations to bear in mind.

- Wooden tubs or large terra-cotta pots are essential, at least 15 inches deep and across. Place broken pieces of clay pots in them to create good drainage; use soil-based compost.
- Use dwarfing rootstocks such as M27 or M9. Without their use, growing apples in pots is not practical.
- To ensure pollination (and the subsequent development of fruit) choose a "family" tree, where 3–4 different yet compatible varieties have been grafted onto one rootstock. Alternatively, it is necessary to plant—in separate pots—several varieties.
- Buy a two-year-old tree and plant and stake it.
- It is best trained as a pyramid, which means in winter cutting back the leading shoot to about 6 inches from where it developed from the trunk. Additionally, cut back sideshoots near the plant's top to 6–8 inches from the trunk, and those near the base to 10–12 inches from the trunk.
- During the second winter, cut back all branches to about 6–8 inches from where they developed during the previous growing period.
- During the first year, allow 2–3 fruits to develop; in later years, expect about 10 pounds of fruit.

Varieties to try include:

- 'Early Harvest': eating and culinary variety; pick apples in summer; they are ready for eating in summer and early autumn.
- 'Egremont Russet': eating variety; pick apples in early autumn; they will be ready for eating from mid-autumn to early winter.
- 'Golden Delicious': eating variety; pick apples in late summer; they will be ready for eating during late summer and early autumn.
- 'Granny Smith': eating variety; pick apples in autumn, ready for eating from early winter.
- 'James Grieve': eating variety; pick apples in early autumn, ready for eating in early and mid-autumn.

Figs

Figs require a warm climate and a sheltered position. Embryonic fruits develop in the summer and are harvested during the following year. A fig is ready for picking when the stalk weakens and the fruit hangs freely.

Peaches

A warm position is essential for peaches. Test each fruit individually for picking; cup each one in the palm of your hand and twist—if the stalk easily parts from the branch, this means that the fruit is ready.

Strawberries

Strawberries are the most popular fruits for growing in a variety of containers, from hanging-baskets to planters and barrels. Regularly check fruits for picking. This should be done in the morning, when they are dry and have colored all over.

PEACHES IN LARGE POTS

Apart from shelter from cold wind, there are a few other essentials.

- Position in the warmth of a sun-drenched wall.
- For ease of pruning, grow as a bush.
- Use a dwarfing rootstock such as Pixy. It produces a tree 6–7 feet high in a tub or large pot.
- Select a relatively hardy variety, such as 'Belle of Georgia' (for picking mid-summer) or 'Elberta' (for picking during late summer).
- Protect flowers in spring from frost and birds, and later protect the ripening fruits from birds.
- It is essential that you hand-pollinate the flowers.

FIGS IN LARGE POTS

Unless their roots are constricted, figs are rampant and produce leafy growth at the expense of fruits. Therefore, they are ideal for growing in containers. Here are a few essentials for success.

- In spring, put a young fig plant in a large tub and position in the shelter and warmth of a wall.
- Grow the fig as a small bush (rather than as a fan).
- During winter, protect shoots and young figs from frost.
- Repot plants every 2–3 years.
- Select varieties such as 'Brown Turkey' (for picking late summer and early autumn) and 'Celeste' (for picking early to late summer).

BLUEBERRIES IN LARGE POTS

These are increasingly popular and easy to grow in large containers. Here are a few clues to success with them.

- Choose a tub or large wooden box at least 1½ feet deep and wide. Good drainage is essential.
- Use ericaceous (acid) compost and plant in spring. They grow to about 4 feet high.
- Use the popular and widely grown variety 'Bluecrop'.
- Attractive white flowers, tinged with pink, appear in spring, and fruits follow in mid-summer.
- Protect fruits from birds and, preferably, water with rainwater.

Choosing and buying plants

Much of the success of growing plants in containers—as well as in gardens—is to buy healthy, well-established, pest-and-disease-free plants that will quickly become established and create magnificent displays. Summer-flowering bedding plants especially have a limited time to become established before they are expected to drench containers in color. The selection of bulbs for spring display also needs care; inferior bulbs never produce good displays.

A small, decorative, terra-cotta trough introduces extra color and interest to a patio or to a gravel path like this one.

WHERE TO BUY PLANTS

Many places sell plants for putting in containers, and these include garden centers, nurseries, supermarkets, and local stores. There are also garden clubs and stalls in markets, and plants can be purchased by mail order. Wherever you obtain your plants, however, buy only the best quality—an inexpensive buy is a costly experience if it does not produce a good display several months later.

Garden centers

Buying from garden centers is popular and plants can be checked before you buy. Additionally, advice is often possible if you are in doubt about what to buy. They usually have a wide range of plants which are inspected daily to ensure they are healthy and attractive.

Nurseries

Plants bought from nurseries have usually been grown on that site and their qualities and attributes are well known to the nursery staff. For that reason, specialized advice is usually available. Some nurseries specialize in specific plants, such as bamboos, trees, and shrubs, while others have a general range of plants.

Mail order

This is an ideal way to buy plants if you are housebound or have transportation difficulties. Plants are advertised in regional and local newspapers, and glossy magazines. For quality, it is necessary to rely on the integrity of the supplier. Check plants immediately after delivery and notify suppliers of any problems.

WHAT TO LOOK FOR

GOOD HEALTH	COMMON PROBLEMS	RARE PROBLEMS
Before buying any plant, check that it is growing strongly and looks bright and healthy. Here are a few clues when inspecting plants:	*Most problems arise from neglect and result from the often large numbers of plants on sale in spring and early summer and the limited time to look after them. Therefore, before buying, remember:*	*Garden centers and nurseries have reputations to consider and invariably endeavor to ensure that customers are happy with their plants and will make repeat visits. Presentation as well as quality is all-important to them. Yet this does not apply to all suppliers.*
• Compost should be moist but not waterlogged. Plants can wilt from having dry compost as well as if it is excessively wet and the roots are inactive and perhaps decaying.	• Where summer-flowering bedding plants are sold in strips or complete flats, check that they are all in a saleable condition. Plants near edges are most vulnerable.	• Dried edges to leaves indicate earlier watering neglect, even though the compost may now be moist.
• Leaves and flowers should be free from blemishes and signs of pests and diseases. Always look under the leaves.	• Where roots of summer-flowering bedding plants only slightly protrude out of the container, it is not a problem; but where they roam farther this means breaking them off when removing plants from the container.	• Chewed leaves and stems, as well as mottled patches, show that chewing and sucking pests have been present. Look under leaves.
• Don't buy spindly and weak plants—they never recover and later may leave gaps in container displays.	• Where roots of container-grown shrubs are matted and protruding out of the container, this indicates neglect and that the plant may have suffered.	• Wilting stems and leaves may indicate the presence of root-chewing pests as well as the need for water—or even too much water.
• Don't buy plants exposed to extremes of temperature or strong wind. They may have been chilled or overheated.		

WHEN TO BUY

The time of the year to buy plants depends on their nature and uses.

- Spring-flowering bulbs: buy during late summer for planting in early autumn. Available from bulb specialists as well as garden centers and local stores.
- Spring-flowering biennials: buy during late summer for planting in early autumn. Available from garden centers, nurseries, and local stores.
- Summer-flowering bedding plants: buy in late spring or early summer and plant as soon as all risk of frost has passed. Available from garden centers, nurseries, and local stores.
- Shrubs and trees: container-grown plants can be bought throughout the year and planted whenever the soil and weather are suitable. However, when they are to be grown in containers, planting is best tackled during spring or early summer. Available from garden centers, nurseries, and local stores.
- Miniature and slow-growing conifers: invariably sold as container-grown plants throughout the year, but best bought and planted into containers during spring or early summer. Available from garden centers, nurseries, and local stores.

GETTING THEM HOME

Getting plants home safely is an early stage in successful container gardening. Here are a few clues to success.

- Ensure there is adequate space in your car for the plants you buy.
- Don't have young children with you.
- Don't have a dog in the car.
- Don't drive fast over pot holes and speed ramps.
- Don't expose plants to drafts.
- Don't leave plants in strong sunlight.

PREPARING CONTAINERS

Getting display containers ready for planting is just as important as preparing plants. Some containers, such as trough-like shells used inside many ornate window boxes, are plain and functional. Others are ornamental and need to be given pre-planting treatment, especially to ensure that they are clean.

Hanging-baskets

← Wash and scrub both wire-framed and plastic types to remove dirt and compost that remains from the previous year. Where there is a drip-tray or self-watering device, ensure it is secure and not blocked. Check supporting chains and fixings, as well as screw-type hooks used to suspend the basket.

Window boxes

← Scrub and clean inner boxes as well as ornate outer ones. Check that drainage holes are free and, if using a new, plastic inner box, remove the drainage plugs. Check that wall brackets are secure—eventually they become loose and need tightening or replacing. Never risk them breaking during summer, especially if the display is secured outside an upstairs room.

Troughs

← Scrub and clean troughs. If formed of reconstituted stone, do not use detergents; instead, use warm water and a soft brush. If the trough is large and in a permanent position, plants close by may have encroached on it; cut them back or remove entirely. Check that drainage holes are free.

Pots, urns, and tubs

← These are varied in shape as well as materials, which range from plastic and glass-fiber to reconstituted stone. Inspect their structure, as well as the positions in which they will eventually be displayed. If made of reconstituted stone and cemented to a plinth, check that is it secure.

Wooden containers

These have varied shapes, from tubs to Versailles planters. Whatever their size and shape, the wood eventually decays and falls apart, especially if constructed of unseasoned, inferior lumber. Sometimes removal and disposal is the only solution. Life expectancy can be extended by repairs, but the best preventative measure is to ensure excess water can drain from the base. Also, standing a tub on 3–4 bricks ensures that water drains freely.

PRE-PLANTING TREATMENT

The treatment that should be given to plants either when you get them home or when they arrive by mail order depends on their type.

- Spring-flowering bulbs: unpack (without mixing up the varieties) and remove the polyethylene covering. Place the bulbs in a cool, dark, vermin-proof drawer or shed.
- Spring-flowering biennials: these are

usually sold as bare-rooted plants in bunches; sometimes the roots are wrapped. Leave them in bunches (to avoid mixing the varieties) and stand these in clean water. Make sure that the roots do not become dry.

- Summer-flowering bedding plants: leave in their containers and stand them outdoors on raised benches to prevent slugs and snails getting at

them. Water the plants thoroughly; leaves should be dry by evening.

- Shrubs and trees: if they have been container-grown, the plants should be placed outdoors on a firm surface and watered several times.
- Miniature and slow-growing conifers: these are invariably sold growing in containers; stand them outdoors on a firm surface and water several times.

Window boxes

*How can I
have color
all year?*

Window boxes are ideal for creating color throughout the year. Three distinct arrangements of plants—spring, summer, and winter—in three separate inner boxes are needed, and by rotating them in an outer window box it is possible to produce uninterrupted color from one season to another. Some window boxes are just planted with summer-flowering displays, but this is not adventurous and does not use a window box to its full potential.

A window box planted with colorful trailing plants such as Petunias can make a striking display in the summer months in an otherwise dull space.

WHAT ARE THE ADVANTAGES OF USING WINDOW BOXES?

Window boxes introduce many design qualities to patio gardens—as well as front yards.
- Color can be provided throughout the year by means of three separate and distinctive displays.
- Displays, although they are mainly appreciated from the outside, can also be seen from indoors and through the relevant windows.
- Fragrant flowers can be positioned near windows, where a wide range of scents can waft indoors.
- Where double window box displays are used—with one box positioned about 9 inches above the other—the area of wall clothed in color is doubled. Remember to check, however, that the lower box can be reached for watering.
- Window boxes help to unify hanging-baskets when positioned on both sides of a window. Color contrasts as well as harmonies are possible between the window box and the hanging-baskets, both to suit each other and to contrast with the background.

SELECTING A WINDOW BOX

Choose a window box that harmonizes with the house. Formal types are needed for clinically designed modern houses, while informal ones are better suited to older houses. The range of materials is wide, and includes wood, plastic, glass-fiber, terra cotta, and reconstituted stone, while the design choice is plain or ornate.

Wooden window boxes

Cedar

Painted pine

Pine log effect

Lattice front

MAKING YOUR OWN WINDOW BOX

Wooden window boxes are easy to construct at home. One formed of ¾-inch thick wood, and with internal measurements of 32 inches long and 8 inches deep and wide, is large enough to accommodate an inner box.

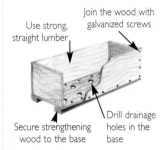

Join the wood with galvanized screws

Use strong, straight lumber

Secure strengthening wood to the base

Drill drainage holes in the base

Other types of window box

Decorated wood

Terra cotta

Plastic lead effect

Metal frame

White-painted steel

Reconstituted stone

Plastic kit

Woven willow

PHILOSOPHY OF USING WINDOW BOXES

- **In autumn**, plant a spring display and place it outdoors in a sheltered position. In spring, the winter display is removed and the spring display put in its place.
- **In early summer**, replace the spring display with a box that

has been planted with a summer-flowering arrangement.
- **In late summer**, remove the summer display and replace it with the winter display which was previously removed from the window box in early spring.

SPRING

Planted in autumn
Mainly formed of bulbs and spring-flowering hardy biennials

SUMMER

Planted in late spring
Mainly formed of summer-flowering bedding plants

WINTER

Planted in late summer
Mainly formed of hardy foliage plants

POSITIONING WINDOW BOXES

For sash windows, window boxes can be positioned directly on strong sills.

For casement windows, position a window box on brackets and slightly below the sill.

Wall spaces between sash windows benefit from window boxes. Ensure watering is possible.

PLANTING WINDOW BOXES

Plants in window boxes can be either planted directly in compost or left in their pots and plunged (see below right). Summer displays are usually planted into compost in an inner box. Remember to check that water can drain away freely through the drainage holes in the base.

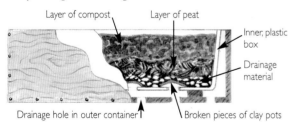

Layer of compost   Layer of peat
Inner, plastic box
Drainage material
Drainage hole in outer container
Broken pieces of clay pots

GOOD WINDOW BOX PLANTS

Window box plants need to be chosen with care. Apart from avoiding plants that are soon buffeted by autumn and winter winds, they must provide reliable displays.

SPRING DISPLAYS:

- English Daisy—see page 22 • EnglishWallflower—see page 22
- Forget-me-not—see page 22 • Polyanthus—see page 22
- Trumpet Daffodils—see page 39 • Tulips—see page 39

For further plants, see pages 22–23.

SUMMER DISPLAYS:

- Calceolarias—see page 17 • Cascade Geraniums—see page 17
- Petunias—see page 19 • Sweet Alyssum—see page 18
- Tuberous-rooted Begonias—see page 17
- Wax Begonias—see page 16

For further plants, see pages 16–20.

WINTER DISPLAYS:

- Small, hardy, evergreen shrubs—see pages 32–33
- Slow-growing and miniature conifers—see pages 34–35
- Trailing evergreen Ivies—see page 23

For further plants, see page 23.

Composts

Whatever the type of compost, it must be clean and free from pests and diseases.

Spring-flowering displays: use well-drained, loam-based compost. This gives plants a firm base that suits spring-flowering bulbs, biennials, and, sometimes, a few small conifers and trailing *Hedera helix* (Ivies).

Summer-flowering displays: peat-based composts, with their ability to retain moisture, are ideal for window boxes that need to support a large number of plants.

Winter displays: use well-drained, loam-based compost for these long-term displays, which are mainly formed of miniature slow-growing conifers, trailing ivies, and small evergreen shrubs.

PLUNGING POTS

Instead of removing their pots, some displays—mainly in winter—can be made by plunging pots in moist peat. This method—in contrast to removing pots and planting soil balls directly into compost—enables flowering plants that cease their display or are damaged by frost to be quickly removed and replaced.

Hanging-baskets

How should I fill a hanging-basket?

When planted, a hanging-basket becomes packed with plants that quickly grow and create a magnificent display. The essential needs of these plants are moisture-retentive compost—kept moist throughout summer—and regular feeding to encourage strong and healthy growth. Therefore, careful planting, using clean compost, is essential. Planting a basket is detailed on the opposite page, together with suggestions for suitable composts.

CREATING BEAUTIFUL BASKET DISPLAYS

Use hanging-baskets to highlight entrances, but make sure that they cannot be knocked.

Mixing and matching flowering and foliage plants in a hanging-basket, as well as color-coordinating them with attractive backgrounds, are ways to get the best out of these popular summer-long features. If planting them yourself is likely to be a time and space problem, established hanging-baskets can be bought from nurseries and garden centers in early summer. Sometimes it is possible to choose specific plants and colors if the order is made early, perhaps in mid-winter. To get them home safely, stand large baskets in the top of a round bowl.

Ornate, basket-weave containers have a dainty and rustic appearance.

GUIDE TO SELECTING HANGING-BASKETS

Wire-framed hanging-baskets range in width from 10 to 18 inches. Choose one with plastic-coated wire. Bowl-shaped plastic hanging-baskets have solid sides, which help with moisture retention. Additionally, some of these baskets have drip-trays built into their bases, and these are ideal for displaying plants in porches and conservatories.

Wire round-bottomed hanging-basket

Wrought-iron-style hanging-basket with open sides

Terra-cotta-style ornately decorated hanging-basket

Plastic hanging-basket with planting pockets and drip-tray

Fit a rounded, plastic container within the basket

DISPLAY POSITIONS

Most hanging-baskets are suspended from wall brackets screwed to a wall. This lets the basket hang freely, with its edge 4–6 inches from the wall. Screwing large hooks into a bargeboard or fascia is possible for one-storied houses (but check they are secure).

Suspend a basket from a wall bracket

Hang a basket from a bargeboard or fascia

Secure a basket to an overhead framework

FIRM FIXINGS

Secure fastenings are essential, as well as rustproof supporting chains. When laden with plants and at the height of summer—and when recently watered—baskets are heavy. Also, wind rocks baskets and loosens weak fixings. Do not hang baskets over sidewalks; excess water drips, and if brackets or chains fail it could be disastrous.

WATERING AND FEEDING TIPS

- Add moisture-retaining additives to the compost (see below).
- Avoid placing baskets in windy positions that will rapidly dry out the compost.
- Place a saucer in the base of the basket (while planting) that will act as a small reservoir.
- If the compost becomes very dry, take down the basket and immerse the compost in water until bubbles cease to rise. Then, let water drain before putting it back in position.
- Add slow-acting fertilizers to the compost while planting the basket.
- Regular feeding is essential—first ensure that the compost is moist. Never apply fertilizers while the compost is dry.

Composts

- Proprietary hanging-basket composts are available and some of these have additives that assist in moisture retention.
- Peat-based composts are better than loam-based types for hanging-baskets, although they are more difficult to remoisten if they have been left to become dry.
- A mixture of equal parts peat-based and loam-based compost is a good compromise; the peat retains moisture and the loam provides food over a longer period.

MOISTURE RETENTION

As an aid to moisture retention in compost, you can add perlite and vermiculite. Earlier, shredded cork was used. Proprietary basket liners (put in place while planting a basket) assist in water retention.

MAKING A BASKET

For an imaginative and attractive basket, create a lattice-work of 9-inch long pieces of 1½-inch wide and 1-inch thick wood by drilling holes in the ends and bolting them together, as shown here. Line the finished basket with sphagnum moss to contain the compost.

SPHAGNUM MOSS OR PLASTIC?

Sphagnum moss is a traditional material for lining wire-framed hanging-baskets. It retains moisture in the compost and prevents it falling out. It is also very attractive. Sphagnum moss is difficult to obtain and in its place hanging-baskets are usually lined with black polyethylene.

PLANTING A BASKET

Plants used in hanging-baskets are easily damaged by frost. Therefore, if planting is tackled before all risk of frost has passed, ensure there is somewhere the basket can be placed, such as a frostproof greenhouse. If left outside, plants can be given slight protection by pushing a few sheets of newspaper between the plants and supporting chains.

l *Place a wire-framed basket in the top of a bucket and line it with black polyethylene. Mold it to the shape of the basket and cut it off 2 inches above the rim. When planting is complete, further trimming is necessary.*

2 *Put a handful of moist peat in the base of the basket, then add compost (see left) to about half the depth of the basket. Gently firm the compost, but take care not to push your fingers through the plastic sheeting.*

3 *Use a sharp knife to make 2-inch long slits in the polyethylene, level with the surface of the compost and about 4 inches apart. Push the roots of trailing plants through each hole and cover and firm them with compost.*

4 *Add more compost and plant a dominant, cascading plant in the center, with the top of its rootball about 1 inch below the basket's rim. Add further plants around it, with trailing types at the edges. Firm the compost.*

5 *When planting is complete, add a thin layer of sphagnum moss (if available) to the surface. This conserves moisture and creates an attractive surface. Leave the basket in the bucket and gently but thoroughly water the compost.*

AFTER-PLANTING CHECKS ...

- Before putting a basket in its display position, inspect it for pests and diseases. Spray if pests such as greenfly are seen—they soon multiply and spread if spraying is neglected.
- If you don't think that you will be able to give regular attention to pest control, insert a few insecticide pins into the compost. Plants absorb the chemicals, which kill sucking and chewing insects.
- If giving regular feeds is going to be a problem, insert slow-release fertilizer sticks into the compost.

Baskets in lobbies and porches

Are houseplants hardy enough for a porch?

Inside porches and lobbies only relatively hardy houseplants are likely to be successful in hanging-baskets, although much depends on whether the area is open to the elements or enclosed by an outer door. Nevertheless, many indoor plants can usually be grown here, and these are described on pages 44–45. Drip-trays are essential parts of indoor hanging-baskets, and plants can either be planted into compost or stood in a flat-based basket (see right).

LOBBY AND PORCH DISPLAYS

The choice of positions for hanging-baskets to be displayed in lobbies and porches depends on their size and, especially, their width.

- Wherever possible, position a hanging-basket away from a door that would direct cold air on plants. However, foliage plants are hardier than most flowering types and, if essential, can be put in a more exposed and cool position.
- Grouping several different plants in the same container creates displays over long periods and several medleys are featured on page 45.
- Narrow lobbies and porches are often able to fit in small, wall-fixed baskets rather than ones suspended from a bracket. Many suitable plants are described on pages 44–45.

GETTING THE DISPLAY RIGHT

When planting an outdoor hanging-basket, most plants are small and perhaps removed from "strips" of plants or bought separately but without an attractive pot. Conversely, plants used in hanging-baskets in lobbies and porches invariably are established in pots. For this reason, it is easier to plan a display in detail before transferring the design and plants to a basket.

- Draw a circle on a piece of paper to the same size and shape of the basket.
- Place a dominant plant in the center of the circle and cluster others around it, in varying positions until an attractive display is created.
- It is an ideal way to use available plants to the best advantage.
- When the design is complete, transfer them to the hanging-basket.

Hanging-baskets introduce added color and vitality to a porch, but make sure they cannot be knocked or prevent doors opening.

... don't get the floor wet

Drip-trays that are integrated into the structure are essential parts of hanging-baskets to be used in lobbies and porches. There are several excellent designs on the market.

PORCH AND LOBBY OPTIONS

Porches and lobbies offer attractive homes for plants in hanging-baskets that have integral drip-trays (see page 54). These areas are usually unheated and porches are often colder and more exposed than lobbies.

In a porch

↗ *During summer, both outdoor hanging-basket plants and hardy houseplants can be used, but in winter hardy foliage plants are better at surviving low temperatures.*

In a lobby

↗ *Medleys of flowering and attractively foliaged houseplants are ideal for lobbies, especially during summer. In winter, give more prominence to those that have attractive foliage.*

PLANTING OPTIONS

There are two options when planting a hanging-basket for a porch or lobby. One is to plant directly into compost; the other is to leave plants in their pots. With both methods, thoroughly water the plants the day before planting. Here are details of tackling both of these methods.

Planting into compost

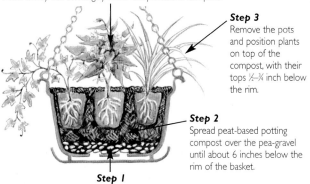

Step 4
Pack and firm compost between plants, as well as slightly over them. Gently but thoroughly water the plants and compost.

Step 3
Remove the pots and position plants on top of the compost, with their tops ½–¾ inch below the rim.

Step 2
Spread peat-based potting compost over the pea-gravel until about 6 inches below the rim of the basket.

Step 1
Thoroughly clean and dry the basket. Then, spread a ¾–1-inch thick layer of pea-gravel over the base.

Leaving pots in place

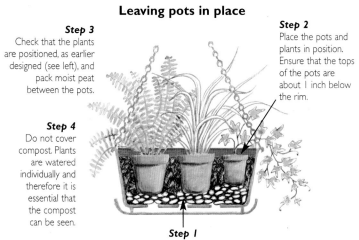

Step 3
Check that the plants are positioned, as earlier designed (see left), and pack moist peat between the pots.

Step 2
Place the pots and plants in position. Ensure that the tops of the pots are about 1 inch below the rim.

Step 4
Do not cover compost. Plants are watered individually and therefore it is essential that the compost can be seen.

Step 1
Select a plastic, flat-bottomed, indoor hanging-basket and spread a 1-inch thick layer of pea-gravel over the base.

WATERING AND FEEDING

Like all other plants in containers, plants in hanging-baskets need regular watering, especially during summer.
- In hanging-baskets where plants are left in their pots it is necessary to check each plant individually to see if the compost is becoming dry. Remember that large plants in small pots need more frequent watering than small plants in large pots. Ensure that plants are not given too much water.
- Where pots have been removed and plants are growing in the same compost, keep the compost evenly moist, but not excessively wet.

Composts

- When planting: where pots are removed, so that plants can be planted into compost, use a peat-based type. To assist in moisture-retention, add some clay granules to the compost.

- Leaving pots in place: where each plant is left in its pot, use moist peat to pack around and between the pots to keep their compost moist and cool, especially when they are to be hung in a warm atmosphere.

FIXING

Use strong fixings. Sometimes, cup-hooks can be screwed into beams in the ceilings of porches and lobbies. Take care, especially in constricted areas, that wall-secured brackets cannot damage eyes. A range of fixings is shown on page 54. Plastic-coated and ornate metal types are available.

FOCAL DISPLAYS

In large lobbies, out-of-the-way corners can be brightened by using groups of plants—some standing on the floor and others in hanging-baskets. Use a combination of plants—mix variegated foliage types and others with flowers. Additionally, use a spotlight to highlight the feature and turn it into a focal point.

REPLACING PLANTS

Where plants are left in their pots, plants can be replaced when they stop being attractive. Take care when doing this not to damage neighboring plants. Before putting a new plant into position, first water the compost and let excess moisture drain.

SMARTENING UP PLANTS

Eventually, hanging-baskets where plants are collectively grown in the same compost need to be smartened up, especially when vigorous plants dominate their neighbors. Sometimes, shoots and branches can be snipped off, but usually it is best to start again. Some plants can be reused, whereas others need to be replaced.

Wall-baskets and mangers

Are wall-baskets and mangers a good choice?

Wall-baskets and mangers are increasingly popular and available in a range of sizes and materials. Mangers are sold in widths from 12 to 28 inches, with increases of about 4 inches. Wire-framed wall-baskets range in width from 9 to 20 inches. Plastic and terra-cotta types are usually more decorative and available in widths from 6 to 10 inches. These are ideal for positioning alongside a small, narrow entrance.

Ornate mangers or wire-framed wall-baskets can be suspended from a sturdy sill where wall coverings such as shingles prevent the drilling of holes. Ensure that all fixings are safe.

Bland and unappealing walls can be given vitality and eye appeal by securing mangers or wall-baskets to them. Throughout the summer months, they can be drenched with color.

DECORATING WALLS

Wall-baskets and mangers can be used to create magnificent displays. They are mainly positioned at waist height and can be displayed in many different places.

- Wide mangers can be used under windows, instead of window boxes. With their rustic appearance they harmonize well with old properties.
- Position small wall-baskets between windows and, perhaps, in combination with a window box or manger underneath a window.
- Small wall-baskets are ideal for positioning on walls at the sides of doors.
- Placed at waist height along a wall, they can introduce extra color to an otherwise bland area.
- They excel when positioned along the fronts of row cottages, where paving abuts the property. Unlike floor-positioned containers, such as tubs and troughs, they enable the area underneath them to be hosed and cleaned without any difficulty.
- Plastic and terra-cotta wall-baskets are ideal for balcony walls, but take care that water cannot mark the wall.

WALL-BASKET OPTIONS

Simple wire basket · Wrought-iron-style basket · Aluminum non-rusting basket

Ornate wire basket · Corner basket · Miniature baskets

MANGER OPTIONS

Simple wire manger · Ornate manger · Miniature manger

PLANTING A WALL-BASKET

When planting a wall-basket or manger, ensure that excess water cannot run out of the back of the container and trickle down a wall.

1 *Hold a wall-basket or manger in place and mark the positions of the securing holes. Drill, insert wall-anchors, and screw the container onto the wall.*

2 *Line the inside with strong, black polyethylene (or two layers of bin-liners). Ensure the back is covered to prevent water getting on the wall and staining it.*

3 *Fill the basket or manger to about half full with compost. Then use a pointed knife to pierce holes in the polyethylene, but only at the front.*

4 *Start planting the basket from the back, putting in some bushy plants that will give height to the display. Firm compost around and over them.*

5 *Add further plants, with trailing types positioned along the front edge. Add and firm further compost until ¾ inch below the rim. Gently water the plants.*

GOOD PLANTS FOR WALL-BASKETS AND MANGERS

Many plants can be used in these types of container, for both spring- and summer-flowering displays. Here are a few clues that will guide you to success.

Spring displays:
• When using Tulips, select short-stemmed types that will not be at risk from blustery, late winter and spring weather.
• *Muscari armeniacum* (Grape Hyacinths) are more tolerant of wind, as are the variegated small-leaved *Hedera helix* (Ivies) so often used in spring displays.

Summer displays:
• Always ensure that the compost is covered with leaves and flowers; bare compost in mangers and wall-baskets is always unappealing.
• Preferably, use dome-shaped and bushy plants, with trailing types at the edges to cloak the container.
• Unlike hanging-baskets, which are admired at shoulder or head height, wall-baskets and mangers are positioned at waist level and therefore are admired from above. Bright-faced, upward-facing flowers are therefore desirable.

WATERING AND FEEDING

• Regular watering and feeding is essential throughout summer. While doing this, however, take care not to stand too close to the display as water may drip from drainage slits made in the container's front.
• During winter, less watering is needed. However, in late winter and early spring regularly check that the compost is lightly moist.

Composts

• Use peat-based compost in wall-baskets, especially for summer displays; but for spring displays planted in early autumn it is better to use well-drained, loam-based compost.

• In large mangers, a mixture of equal parts loam-based and peat-based compost gives good results, especially if the compost is left in the container for a couple of years.

• For a small wall-basket, add moisture-retaining materials to the compost.

AFTERCARE

• In late spring, remove all plants after they cease flowering. Discard biennials, but bulbous types can be planted around other plants such as shrubs in mixed borders.
• In late summer or early autumn, remove summer-flowering displays. Add further compost (as needed) or completely refurbish the basket, and plant a spring-flowering display.

DISPLAY COMBINATIONS

Using color-themed wall-baskets and mangers against color harmonizing and contrasting walls is described on pages 12–13. Here are a couple of combinations of plants to consider, for spring and summer displays.

Spring displays

← These do not have to be packed with rare and expensive plants. Here is a medley of bright-faced Pansies, variegated small-leaved *Hedera helix* (Ivies), and the variegated *Lamium maculatum* 'Album', with mid-green leaves that reveal a central silver stripe.

Summer displays

← For a dramatic two-plant display, use a dominant planting of a red Verbena, with the addition of variegated small-leaved *Hedera helix* (Ivies). This is best seen against a white background, although it will also look good on a red-brick wall.

Stone, glazed, and hypertufa sinks

Do I need a special sink?

Old, shallow, stone sinks are ideal containers for alpine and small rock-garden plants. Miniature and slow-growing conifers are also candidates, as well as miniature bulbs. Deeper, glazed sinks can also be used, but they benefit from being modified and given an aged, rustic appearance (see below). Sinks made of reconstituted stone have a natural appearance, and while some have a traditional sink shape, others have a quarter-circle shape.

MODIFYING A DEEP, GLAZED SINK

Small border plants and culinary herbs can also be used in stone sinks.

- Wash the sink with soap and water and stand it on four bricks that are positioned slightly in from the edges.
- Use an old chisel to scratch the outside and to about 3 inches down the inside edge. Wash and let surfaces dry.
- Paint scratched surfaces with a PVA bonding glue.
- Mix 1 part sharp sand, 1 part cement powder, and 2 parts fine peat (all parts by bulk). Add water and mix to a stiff paste. Before the PVA glue hardens, wear gloves and coat all scratched surfaces with this mixture. Press it firmly against the sides.
- Leave the sink in a dry, cool, frostproof shed for a few weeks.

PREPARING STONE SINKS

Always handle stone sinks with care. They appear strong, but if twisted awkwardly on one edge and knocked, can soon crack. Use soapy water to clean the sink, inside and out, and thoroughly rinse with clean water. Until needed for planting, stand it on bricks.

Another type of container to modify

Redundant fiber-glass shower bases, which are usually about 28 inches square and 6 inches deep, can be coated in the same way as a deep, glazed sink (see left). However, the shell lacks rigidity and needs to be put in its final position before it is modified.

PLANTING SCHEMES FOR STONE SINKS

PLANTING SCHEME

Campanula cochlearifolia

Antennaria dioica

Edraianthus pumilio

Erinus alpinus

Lewisia cotyledon

Hebe buchananii

PLANTING SCHEME

Miniature conifer

Saxifraga cotyledon

Sempervivum tectorum

Sedum spathulifolium

Armeria maritima

Arabis alpina

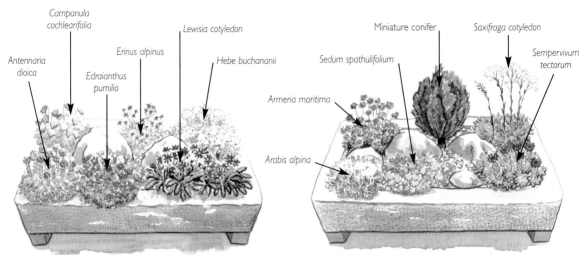

This display drenches the sink in a wide range of colors throughout the spring and summer months.

The addition of a miniature conifer introduces height as well as color to this attractive planting scheme.

PLANTING A STONE SINK

Place a clean stone sink in position, on four strong bricks and with a slight slope to the drainage hole. A warm, sheltered position in good light and away from over-hanging deciduous trees is essential; fallen leaves on top of plants encourage decay.

1 *Crumple a piece of wire-netting and press it firmly into the drainage hole. Then, over the top place a large piece of broken clay pot to prevent compost blocking the hole.*

2 *Cover the base with a 1-inch thick layer of pea-gravel. Then, spread a 1½–2-inch thick layer of granulated peat over the pea-gravel.*

3 *On a large piece of paper, mark the shape of the sink. Place it on the ground and spread out the plants to be planted into the container in an attractive manner.*

4 *Fill and firm the sink with compost to within 1 inch of the rim; use a trowel to do the planting. Firm the compost and spread stone chippings over the top.*

COMPOST FOR SINK GARDENS

A well-drained, loam-based compost combined with extra sharp sand and peat is suitable for most plants in a sink garden. For lime-hating plants, omit the chalk in the compost or buy a special proprietary mixture for acid-loving plants.

WATERING AND FEEDING TIPS

- From mid-spring to autumn, regularly water the compost, taking care not to excessively splash water on soft, hairy leaves. Do not disturb the pea-gravel, as this helps to keep the compost cool and moist during summer, and prevent heavy rain splashing compost on plants.
- Feeding is not usually necessary as over-lush and rampant plants are not attractive in sinks. However, plants that have been in a sink for several years benefit from a low-nitrogen, granular fertilizer applied in spring and once more in mid-summer. Keep the fertilizer off leaves.

HOW TO MAKE A HYPERTUFA SINK

A hypertufa sink is an exciting feature and not difficult to make. It has a natural, tufa-like appearance and is ideal for alpine plants.
1 Its construction means using a bare piece of firm, level, somewhat clay soil as a mold. Using strings, mark a rectangle 2 feet long and 16 inches wide.
2 With a builder's trowel, carefully remove soil from the area to about 2 inches deep, leaving the sides square and intact.
3 Mark an area 3 inches wide around the original rectangle and, using a trowel, excavate this to 7 inches deep. This creates the mold for the sides.
4 Carefully knock two dowels—about 1 inch thick—into the base. Later, these will be the drainage holes.
5 Prepare hypertufa: by parts, mix 1 of cement powder, 1 of sharp sand, and 4 of clean, moderately dry, granulated peat. Add water to form a stiff but pliable paste.
6 Fill and firm the sides, as well as 1 inch in depth on the top, with the mixture.
7 Place galvanized netting over the top and then a further 1 inch of the mixture. Smooth with a builder's trowel or float. Cover the sink with a protective covering and leave it to set for at least a couple of weeks.
8 Carefully dig out the sink, ease out the pegs, wash it, and place it in its display position. Stand the sink on firm supports such as strong bricks (see above right).

↗ *Hypertufa sinks have an attractive, informal, and rustic appearance.*

↗ *Stand the sink on strong bricks to make plants easier to see, but do not block the drainage holes.*

↗ *During construction (see step 4, left), knock two dowels into the base to create the drainage holes.*

Troughs and planters

What are troughs?

Planters and troughs are versatile containers and range from simple yet effective plastic ones to large and ornate types formed of reconstituted stone. Others are made of wood, terra cotta, or glass-fiber. In size they also vary, from 20-inch long troughs, that can be placed on walls and floors of balconies and create homes for ephemeral plants, to large and dominant types that provide growing places for more permanent plants, including small shrubs.

SELECTING A TROUGH OR PLANTER

Wooden trough incorporating a trellis

Ornate oval planter

Reconstituted stone trough

Gothic-style resin planter

The practical qualities required of a trough are that it is well drained, creates a secure base for plants, and holds enough compost to provide food and moisture for plants. Additionally, there are esthetic factors, such as ensuring that the trough harmonizes with its position in a garden. There are many different designs, both clinical and ornate.

USING TROUGHS

Troughs are versatile and can be used in many different positions in a garden, as well as on balconies. However, wherever they are positioned, ensure that water can drain freely from the trough yet not inconvenience people. Here are a few places to consider.

↗ *Brighten up any dull floor areas that are close to walls.*

Planting summer-flowering plants

As soon as the risk of frost has passed in late spring or early summer, summer-flowering plants can be planted. Place broken pieces of clay pot over drainage holes, then a layer of pea-gravel. Add compost and set the plants in position. Firm the compost and gently but thoroughly water the compost.

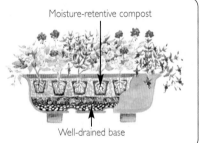

Moisture-retentive compost

Well-drained base

↗ *At the edges of balconies, let plants trail through the bars.*

TROUGHS ON LEGS

As well as placing troughs at patio level, or at the sides of balconies, they look good when raised up on legs. Here are some ideas to try.

• Ornate, wrought-iron designs are available from garden centers and mail-order catalogs and usually display troughs at about 2 feet high. Because the supporting framework is attractive, the trough can be plain so that it will not compete for attention.

• Rustic wooden troughs can be placed on strong wooden legs, again with an informal shape.

• Reconstituted stone troughs are perfectly complemented by ornate plinths in a similar material. Ensure that they are load-bearing and will support the trough when filled with plants and moist compost.

COMPOSTS FOR TROUGHS

• Summer-flowering displays: peat-based composts are ideal. They provide a moisture-retentive medium and some fertilizers. However, you will need to feed plants throughout summer.

• Spring displays: use loam-based compost for bulbs and spring-flowering biennials.

• Perennial displays: use well-drained loam-based compost for long-term flowers. Add extra sharp sand to the mixture.

↗ *Liven up uninteresting courtyard walls with a wall-secured trough.*

Raised beds

Raised beds are permanent features in gardens, constructed usually of bricks but occasionally strong wood. They are often an integral part of a patio or terrace and sometimes have built-in sitting and relaxing positions as part of their design. Raised beds enable plants to be displayed throughout the year and are especially useful where the soil is not suitable for the plants you want to grow—too chalky or too acid, or even if badly drained.

What are raised beds?

CHOICE OF RAISED BEDS

Reconstituted stone blocks

Rustic log-rolls

Brick bed with capping

Low brick wall

Raised beds must be strongly constructed and harmonize with the nature of the garden. Log-rolls and reconstituted stone exude informality, while brick-edged beds have a formal appearance. Well-drained compost is essential, and a mixture of clean, weed-free topsoil and sharp sand is suitable. Ensure that water in compost in a raised bed can easily drain away; the build-up of water in compost can eventually cause the sides of the raised bed to collapse.

Mediterranean-style feature with raised beds. Colored gravel creates extra interest.

AN L-SHAPED RAISED BED

➜ Tall, raised beds are ideal for gardeners in wheelchairs or for those who are unable to bend down easily. Ensure that the brickwork is safe and that the bricks are well bonded together. Leave some weeping holes in the sides for the free drainage of water from the compost.

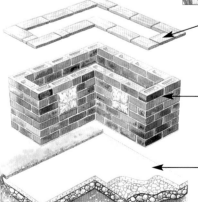

A capping along the wall's top is essential to ensure that rainwater does not enter the bricks and vertical bonds, thus weakening the structure.

By constructing an L-shaped raised bed, a much stronger feature will be created than would be the case with a long and narrow type.

Strong foundations are essential to ensure a long life for the raised bed. Wide foundations are better than narrow ones for each wall.

STONE RAISED BED

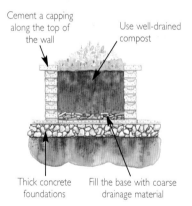

Cement a capping along the top of the wall

Use well-drained compost

Thick concrete foundations

Fill the base with coarse drainage material

Permanent raised beds are ideal for constructing on an existing patio that has a strong, thick base. Such beds can be built of bricks, reconstituted stone, or concrete blocks, and may be positioned exactly to your preferred design. For ease of construction, a square or rectangular shape is always best, and this should be built to a height not exceeding 2½ feet. Remember to leave small weeping holes between the lower parts of the brickwork to let any excess water escape freely.

Pots, tubs, and urns

How should I display pots, tubs, and urns?

Pots, tubs, and urns are popular features on patios and terraces, as they can be grouped to create varied displays that suit the shape and background of the area. A couple of dominant urns at the top or bottom of a flight of steps can also be dramatic. If planted with light-colored foliage or bright flowers, they help to define the edges of the steps during late-summer evenings. Herb planters are ideal for displays in cottage and informal gardens.

PLANTING A SHRUB IN A TUB

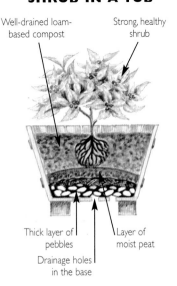

Well-drained loam-based compost

Strong, healthy shrub

Thick layer of pebbles

Layer of moist peat

Drainage holes in the base

Shrubs and small trees are long-term plants in tubs and therefore need careful planting.

1 Select a large, strong tub with drainage holes drilled in its base. Stand the tub on three strong bricks.
2 Form a layer of large pebbles in the base to ensure the drainage holes do not become blocked. Add a 2-inch layer of moist peat.
3 Add loam-based compost and firm it to form a slight mound.
4 Remove the container from the shrub (watered during the previous day) and position it on the mound. The top of the soil ball should be about 1½ inches below the tub's rim.
5 Add further compost and firm it around the soil ball. The compost, when potting is complete, should be 1 inch below the rim.
6 Lightly but thoroughly water the compost to settle it around the roots.

POT, TUB, AND URN OPTIONS

➔ *The range of attractive containers for plants is impressively wide.*

Large plastic pot

Terra-cotta 'long Toms'

Flared-shape terra-cotta pot

Decorated glazed pot

Glazed ceramic pot

Glazed ceramic pot

Stone-effect pot

Terra-cotta pot

Strawberry or herb planter

Half-barrel

Decorative lead-effect tub

Large handmade terra-cotta urns

Victorian architectural "vase" on a plinth

Wall pot

Wall bracket for three pots

Wall bracket for one pot

Decorative pot

Modern aluminum pot

PLANTING A HERB PLANTER

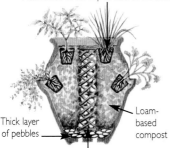

Plant herbs in the top as well as the sides

Thick layer of pebbles

Loam-based compost

Wire-netting tube filled with pebbles

Herbs remain in planters for several years, until they outgrow the container.
1 Place a clean planter in its display position. Stand it on three bricks so that drainage holes are not blocked.
2 Form a layer of large pebbles in the base. Then, roll a piece of wire-netting to form a 3-inch wide tube. Stand it in the center of the planter and with its base on the pebbles. Fill it with pebbles. Fill the base of the planter with loam-based compost to the level of the lowest planting hole.
3 Push the roots of a herb through the hole and onto the compost. Add and firm compost around them; then add further compost. In turn, put a herb in each hole and firm compost around its roots.

PLANTING DAFFODILS IN A SINGLE LAYER

Position bulbs about 1½ inches apart

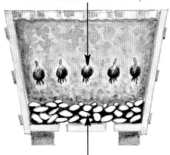

Thick layer of coarse drainage material

Large, golden-faced, Trumpet Daffodils create magnificent displays in spring. To achieve this, bulbs need to be planted in early autumn.
1 Thoroughly clean a large tub and check that drainage holes are not blocked. Position the tub on 3–4 bricks and in its display position.
2 Add a 2-inch layer of coarse drainage material to the base, then firm loam-based compost until 8 inches below the tub's top.
3 Space out healthy bulbs on the compost, leaving about 1½ inches between them. Then add further compost—without disturbing the bulbs—until 1 inch below the tub's rim. Gently but thoroughly water the compost.

PLANTING DAFFODILS IN A DOUBLE LAYER

When Daffodil bulbs are planted in two layers, an even more dramatic and colorful display is created.
1 Prepare a tub in the same way as for a single layer (see left).
2 Add and firm compost to 8 inches below the tub's top. Space out the bulbs, about 3 inches apart, on top of the compost.
3 Trickle and firm compost over them to just below their necks. Then, position a further row of bulbs between them.
4 Add and firm further compost to within 1 inch of the top. Gently but thoroughly water the compost.

Position bulbs in two layers

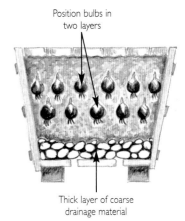

Thick layer of coarse drainage material

HOW TO MAKE A WOODEN PLANTER

⬇ ↘ A low, wooden planter is easy and quick to construct —and if second-hand lumber is available it will also be inexpensive. Don't make it more than 12–15 inches high, as it will then lose rigidity. Indeed, a strong base is essential to give it structural support and a long life.

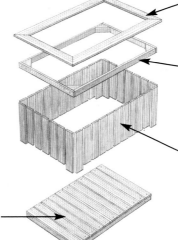

Step 4
Screw a framework of wood to the upper edge to form a cap.

Step 3
Construct a framework of wood to the same size as the base. Nail or screw this to the tops of the side planks.

Step 2
Cut the side planks to length and then nail or screw them to the base. Ensure that they fit closely together.

Step 1
Cut strong planks to form a base. Nail or screw the planks to a framework of side and end wood that will give the base extra rigidity and form supports for the sides.

Container water features

How can I create a miniature water garden?

Few features on patios create as much interest as miniature water gardens in tubs and deep stone sinks. Metal casks are sometimes used, but the temperature of water in them fluctuates throughout summer and takes a dive in autumn. Wooden tubs are the best containers as the water's temperature is then more stable. Be prepared to remove fish from a miniature water garden in autumn, perhaps putting them in a garden pond.

USING A TUB

Select a large, deep, clean tub and place it in its display position. Fill the tub with water and check for any leaks. If it is not watertight, line it with black polyethylene (cut off level with the top). Fill with clean water. Put in water plants in late spring or early summer. Plant them in individual plastic-mesh containers; with Waterlilies, stand the pot on a few bricks so that the pads float. As the plants grow, gradually remove the bricks. Regularly check that the water level is up to the rim. In summer, water soon evaporates and the level drops.

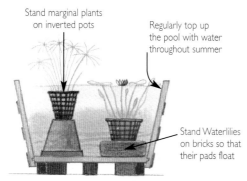

Stand marginal plants on inverted pots

Regularly top up the pool with water throughout summer

Stand Waterlilies on bricks so that their pads float

↗ *Half-barrels are easily converted into miniature water features for display on a patio, but they must be watertight.*

USING A STONE SINK

Water features in stone sinks soon capture attention, but because of the shallowness of the container only small Waterlilies and other plants are practical (see right). Also, because the water's temperature plummets in a stone sink

(although less than in a metal container), it is usually necessary to remove all fish (if present) and plants in autumn and to place them in a cold greenhouse. Rapid temperature fluctuations soon distress fish.

More container ideas

Stone sinks or troughs create superb water features

Concrete dishes are ideal for displays of water plants

Galvanized metal containers make distinctive features

FOLIAGE DISPLAYS IN SMALL CONTAINERS

Small containers—some of metal and others terra-cotta—can be used for summer displays of miniature water plants. If the container is small, put only one plant in it, rather than a collection. In autumn, move the plants and containers to a cold greenhouse, where they will be safe from frost.

Small containers hold insufficient water for fish, but they are ideal for creating displays of water plants.

Barrels

Select a barrel with care, and use only genuine half-barrels with metal hoops and shaped staves—rather than one of the badly made and inferior imitations that are available.

Look for a genuine oak half-barrel with iron hoops. Drive in screws just below the hoops, to hold them in place. Soak the barrel in water until the wood swells within the hoops, making the barrel watertight.

Oak staves angled so that they fit together

Iron hoops; screw them in place to prevent them slipping

COMPOST FOR WATER PLANTS

The best compost for water plants is a heavy loam that has been enriched with a sprinkling of bonemeal to encourage rapid root development. Ensure that the loam is free from decaying debris, such as old roots. After planting, add a layer of clean pea-gravel on the top of the container to prevent the soil being disturbed and clouding the water.

WATER-GARDEN PLANTS FOR TUBS AND SINKS

The key to success with Waterlilies and other water plants in small containers such as tubs, half-barrels, and sinks is to select only those that are likely to grow well in a limited amount of space. The Waterlilies suggested below are either dwarf or small varieties that will happily grow in water that is up to 10 inches deep. As soon as any water plant starts to dominate its container, lift it out and replace it with a smaller one that is more in proportion.

Miniature Waterlilies

Nymphaea 'Laydekeri Lilacea'   *Nymphaea 'Paul Hariot'*   *Nymphaea 'Sioux'*   *Nymphaea 'Pygmaea Helvola'*

Water plants

Carex elata 'Aurea' (also known as Carex stricta 'Bowles' Golden')   *Schoenoplectus lacustris tabernaemontani 'Zebrinus' (also known as Scirpus zebrinus)*   *Iris laevigata 'Variegata'*   *Typha minima*

HOW TO BUILD A BUBBLING URN FEATURE

You need a plastic sump for the reservoir, a ceramic pot or urn (shape and size to suit), a small pump, about 10 feet of water-supply pipe, a sheet of wire mesh, and a bucket of cobblestones.

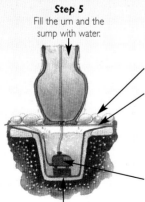

Step 5
Fill the urn and the sump with water.

Step 4
Cover the mesh and pipes with a display of rocks and cobblestones, so that the pipes are hidden.

Step 3
Cover the sump with wire mesh and set the urn in position on top of it. Run the water-supply pipe into the urn.

Step 2
Put the pump in the reservoir and protect the cable with a length of water-supply pipe. Connect the water-supply pipe to the pump.

Step 1
Dig a hole for the sump. Set it in place with sand packed all around it.

HOW TO BUILD A WALL-MASK WATERSPOUT

If you have a patio with a brick wall at one side, you can have a wall-mask waterspout. Use a ready-made trough or tank, or build a brick reservoir to match the wall. If drilling holes through the wall is not an option, mount copper water pipe to the face of the wall and conceal it with foliage.

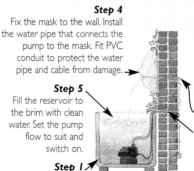

Step 4
Fix the mask to the wall. Install the water pipe that connects the pump to the mask. Fit PVC conduit to protect the water pipe and cable from damage.

Step 3
Sit the pump in the reservoir and run the cable and water pipe through the hole. Drill another hole in the wall at the point where you want the mask to go.

Step 5
Fill the reservoir to the brim with clean water. Set the pump flow to suit and switch on.

Step 2
Drill a hole through the wall, just above the reservoir, big enough to take the water pipe and the pump cable.

Step 1
Position a stone trough or a metal tank; alternatively build a brick reservoir.

Growing-bags on patios

*How do
I use a
growing-bag?*

Growing-bags are versatile and functional containers that create instant homes for flowering and food plants. However, the relatively shallow depth of the compost suits only those plants with fibrous or short roots. Nevertheless, there are many plants to use and places to position them, including near kitchen doors and planted with culinary herbs, on flat roofs and cloaked with trailing flowers, on patios and planted with tomato plants.

THRIFTY GARDENING!

Growing-bags are not single-use containers. As well as providing homes for many and varied plants—from vegetables and herbs to flowering plants—during one season, they can be reused the following year. Even after that season, the compost can be removed and scattered on beds and borders in order to improve the soil.

PREPARING A GROWING-BAG

The compost in growing-bags when stacked in garden centers becomes compressed. Therefore, before using a growing-bag, thorough preparation is needed (see page 47). Additionally, placing the bag on a wooden pallet enables it to be easily moved when planted, as well as making it more difficult for slugs and snails to reach the plants.

↗ On patios, support is needed for tomato plants

↗ Reduce risk from slugs by raising the bag off the ground

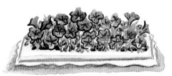
↗ Many flowering plants are ideal for a growing-bag

Growing tomatoes in growing-bags

Plant three cordon types (single, upright stems) in a standard growing-bag. Supports are essential—proprietary metal types are available, but homemade types fashioned from bamboo canes and wires are possible. In a greenhouse, it is possible to push bamboo canes right through the growing-bag and into the soil beneath it. The tops of the canes can be tied to a supporting framework of canes and wires. Pushing canes all the way through a growing-bag in this way ensures that any excess moisture is able to escape.

For growing other vegetables in growing-bags, see pages 46–47. For detailed information on growing potatoes in growing-bags, see right.

MULTI-PLACE CONTAINERS

Few plant containers are as versatile as growing-bags. As well as being placed on a patio or terrace and used for vegetables, they are ideal for introducing summer-flowering plants to the tops of flat roofs, either on home extensions or on garages. Put bushy plants in them, as well as trailing types that will cloak the sides.

Watering plants positioned on the tops of roofs is difficult and proprietary fittings for hosepipes are available. Additionally, a hosepipe when secured by wires to a strong bamboo cane, and with a bent end, enables easy watering.

Growing potatoes in growing-bags

Potatoes can be grown in special potato-growing containers, as well as in large pots (see pages 46–47), but they can also be easily cultivated in growing-bags on a patio. Follow the directions given below.

- In early to mid-spring, prepare a growing-bag; thoroughly shake the bag in order to loosen the compost. Place the growing-bag on a patio or pallet and cut eight, equally spaced, 3–4-inch long, cross-slits in the top. Do not cut away any of the plastic. If the compost is dry, water it thoroughly through the slits.

- Into each slit, push one healthy tuber of an early potato variety, so that it is near the base of the growing-bag and covered with compost.

- Fold back the slits so that light is excluded.

- Regularly check that the compost is moist. However, do not add too much water.

- Shoots arise from the slits and if there is a risk of frost, cover them at night with newspaper.

- When you are ready for an early crop of young potatoes, pull back one of the slits and harvest the tubers.

- There is no need to harvest all of the potatoes at the same time; but fold back the plastic, especially if frost is forecast over the next few days.

Planting pockets and shelves

Unusual yet practical features can be built into patios to create extra color. These range from a few bricks, pavers, or paving slabs left out of a patio floor to provide ground-level growing spaces, to alcoves and recesses carefully fitted into walls and screens. The sides of garden steps can also be made more exciting, with plants in pots positioned along them. All of these features make a patio unique, more interesting, and an extension of your home.

Can I create extra patio color?

Rustic containers, imitating hollowed tree trunks, are novel.

Planting pockets on walls provide opportunities for small plants.

Designer gaps in walls are ideal for small, cascading plants.

Bricks or pavers omitted from patios create spaces for plants.

PLANTING POCKETS

Planting pockets left in a patio's floor are ideal for small, low, creeping plants, including thyme and other cottage-garden plants often planted between natural stone paving. However, take care after snowfalls not to stand on them, nor to clear snow and ice by using a shovel or scattering salt over the area—it soon kills them.

POUCH GARDENING

These are exciting containers for annual patio plants and can be fixed to walls and fences. Basically, they are black plastic tubes which hold compost and into which trailing and bushy plants can be planted. Suitable plants include trailing Lobelias, Pansies, Patience Plants, trailing Petunias, and Verbenas. You can raise the plants yourself or buy them from garden centers or nurseries. It is also possible to grow culinary herbs in pouches, which is ideal for small gardens.

Alcoves

Small alcoves and recesses are ideal for containers.

Recesses where a garden seat for two can be positioned create romantic opportunities, especially when cloaked with fragrant climbers such as *Lonicera* (Honeysuckle) and *Jasminum officinale* (Common Jasmine). Rustic trellises and arbors often have arches built into them, while screen-block walling is sufficiently versatile to have plant-cloaked recesses. You could try covering them with *Clematis montana* (Mountain Clematis), which is sufficiently vigorous to drench them in leaves, with pretty flowers being produced during late spring and early summer.

In addition to large alcoves for seats and, perhaps, benches, small ones (see left) are popular for displaying pots and troughs. If the area is shallow, use upright plants that can be highlighted by a rounded arch.

SHELVES FOR CONTAINERS

As well as constructing recesses in walls so that plants can be put in them, consider leaving a brick or tile projecting so that you can place a plant on it. Protruding bricks built into walls alongside garden steps are attractive, but ensure that the flight of steps is sufficiently wide so that arms do not knock against them.

Protruding bricks from walls make perfect ledges for small pot plants.

BENCHES

Benches with soil constrained by bricks or old railroad ties create unusual features; at seat level, sow grass seed or plant Thyme. An alternative is to plant the non-flowering and low-growing form of Chamomile, *Chamaemelum nobile* 'Treneague' (also known as *Anthemis nobilis* 'Treneague'). It needs little trimming and when the foliage is bruised reveals a refreshing Chamomile-like redolence.

Wheelbarrows

How practical is a wheelbarrow?

Part of the pleasure of container-gardening is creating unusual containers for plants, and few are as captivating as a wheelbarrow. Old wooden wheelbarrows, as well as nonindustrial metal types, create superb homes for summer-flowering plants, especially when painted and positioned against a wall in a contrasting or harmonizing color. Drainage holes in the base are essential to ensure that the compost does not become waterlogged.

A wheelbarrow bursting with summer color creates a fine focal point in a garden.

PLANTING A WHEELBARROW

- Check that the barrow is sound (see below), then put it in its display position.
- To prevent the wood in the base decaying (or the metal rusting), line the whole area with a layer of polyethylene. Puncture it to create drainage holes, matching the positions of those in the wooden or metal base.
- Add a thick layer of pebbles to ensure excess water escapes from the compost.
- Fill and firm the barrow with well-drained, loam-based compost. If the barrow is large, add extra sharp sand.
- Start planting in the middle of the barrow, using dominant plants; work outward until trailing types are positioned around the outside.
- Trim the polyethylene level with the top when planting is complete.
- Gently but thoroughly water the plants. If there is still a risk of frost, cover the plants with newspaper at night to protect them.

MAKING A MINIATURE WOODEN WHEELBARROW

Rather than making a full-sized wooden wheelbarrow, it is much easier to construct a miniature one about 12 inches high, 11 inches wide, and 35 inches long.
For this, you will require the following items:
- five sides to form a box (plus 26 galvanized screws);
- two legs (plus 2 galvanized screws for each);
- two handles (in marine plywood), with bolt-size holes in the wheel-end;
- one wheel (made of thick, marine plywood), with a large central hole, drilled and with two washers;
- one bolt (for fixing the wheel).

Adding gnomes

To complete this diminutive and unusual feature, position a few statues of gnomes all around the miniature wheelbarrow. Choose statues that have accompanying containers, in which you can grow flowering plants.

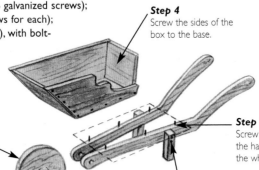

Step 4
Screw the sides of the box to the base.

Step 3
Screw the base of the box to the handles, leaving room for the wheel to turn.

Step 2
Position the wheel and, using the bolt and washers, secure it between the handles, which also form the main supporting framework.

Step 1
Screw the handles to the legs.

CHECKING A WHEELBARROW

Always check wheelbarrows thoroughly in spring before they are filled with compost and put in their display positions.
- Inspect wheel brackets as well as leg and handle fixings. For wooden barrows, metal brackets can be screwed into place, while for metal types tightening up bolts is usually all that is needed.
- If wheel mountings have rusted to a point when they are useless, barrows can be put into position and supported with a few ornate bricks or a strong piece of wood for the duration of summer.

REUSING OTHER CONTAINERS

- Three car tires wired together in a stack and painted white create an unusual feature. Put summer-flowering plants in a plastic bucket (with holes in its base) and position on bricks placed in the center of the tires.

- In coastal areas, a small old rowboat can become home to plants in containers.

Barrels and casks

Growing strawberries in a large barrel creates an attractive feature on a patio, and one that is sure to capture people's attention. A bonus is that strawberries grown in barrels are not usually at risk from the attentions of snails and slugs. Birds are attracted to them, but netting can be spread over the barrel when the fruits are ripening. In areas where the soil is heavy and continually wet, strawberry plants in barrels have a better chance of survival.

Why grow strawberries in a barrel?

PREPARING A STRAWBERRY BARREL

A strong barrel, with the staves (wooden parts) and metal bands in place and undamaged, is essential for long-term life. Clean the barrel, inside and out, with soapy water, then thoroughly rinse. Here are the steps in preparing your barrel.

Step 2
Between the metal bands drill a series of ½–¾-inch wide holes. Then, use a keyhole saw to widen them to about 2 inches. Smooth the edges of the holes.

Step 1
Turn the barrel upside down and drill ¾–1-inch wide drainage holes in the base. Check that the wood is strong enough to support compost.

Step 5
Fill the tube with coarse pebbles, then add compost to the level of the lowest hole. Systematically, put a strawberry plant into each hole and add more compost. Put a few strawberry plants in the top. Water the compost.

Step 4
Roll 1-inch mesh wire-netting into a tube 4–5 inches wide, and long enough to stand on pebbles in the base and rise to just below the barrel's top.

Step 3
Position the barrel upright and place on four stout bricks. Check that the top of the barrel is level; fill the base with 4–6 inches of large pebbles.

DISPLAYING A CASK ON A TRESTLE

Preparation

- Thoroughly clean the cask, then rinse with water.
- On one side, drill four groups of three holes in the metal bands, forming a 14-inch square. Screw the metal bands in place.
- Drill four 1½-inch holes, 12 inches apart and forming an approximate square, in the cask's side. Use a keyhole saw to cut the wood and link them.
- Use a hacksaw to cut the metal bands and open the "window."
- Drill drainage holes on the opposite side.
- Place the cask in the trestle. Fill its base with pebbles, then compost and set plants in place.

Planting options

Casks look good when planted with bushy, as well as trailing, summer-flowering plants. For a display throughout the year, however, drench the planting window with *Sempervivum* plants (Houseleeks). There are many to choose from, including the Hen-and-chicken Houseleek, Common Houseleek, and Cobweb Houseleek.

Compost for barrels

Because ornamental barrels are long-term features, use well-drained, loam-based compost to which extra sharp sand has been added. Do not use soft sand. Peat-based composts are not suitable as they tend to compress and, eventually, exclude air and reduce drainage.

Caring for container plants

How easy is it to care for my plants?

Plants grown in containers need regular attention, especially summer-flowering displays in hanging-baskets, wall-baskets, and window boxes, where plants are positioned close together in order to create instant, dense, and colorful displays. More permanent plants, such as shrubs and trees, also need care, especially during winter when frost and snow can be a problem. Spring-flowering bulbs planted in tubs are usually trouble-free, however.

FRESH TAP WATER OR FROM A WATER-BUTT?

Wherever possible, use fresh water taken directly from a main supply. In winter, of course, the temperature will be low, but as most watering is done during the summer on hanging-baskets, window boxes, and wall-baskets, this is not a factor to consider. In earlier years, using water stored in a water-butt was recommended. However, water-butts filled with rainwater channelled off roofs may, in some locations, be contaminated by micro-organisms and impurities.

WATERING PLANTS

Hanging-baskets

Plants in hanging-baskets soon suffer if watering is neglected. Initially, plants flag and wilt, with flowers being the first to suffer and leaves and stems soon following, the whole plant looking unsightly. If neglect continues, there arrives a time when whatever the amount of water given to plants, they will not recover. Therefore, the skill in watering hanging-baskets is at all times to keep the compost evenly moist, but never waterlogged.

There are several ways to water hanging-baskets (see below). Standing on a stool or stepladder can be dangerous, especially if they are placed on uneven ground and when the basket is high up. Therefore, it is far better to use hosepipe fittings that enable baskets to be watered from ground level.

◤ Proprietary fittings for hosepipes enable water to be gently trickled on compost in hanging-baskets. These have plastic tubing with a bent end, so that water is not wasted and can be directed into the basket. Some pieces of equipment have trigger-like mechanisms that enable water to be turned off between each basket, while others just provide a continuous stream of water.

◤ Homemade fittings for hosepipes are easy to make. All that is needed is a strong, 4 foot long bamboo cane and a piece of wire from a metal coat-hanger. Lay the hosepipe alongside the bamboo cane, with 6–8 inches protruding at one end. Cut three, 6-inch long, pieces of wire to secure the pipe to the cane. Use a slightly longer piece to hold the pipe's end in a curve.

◥ Where it is difficult to water a hanging-basket while suspended, it can be taken down and placed in the top of a plastic bucket and water gently trickled onto the compost. While a hanging-basket is in this position, it is possible to water the compost several times to ensure it is thoroughly moist. Let excess moisture drain before putting the basket back.

◥ If the compost in a hanging-basket becomes very dry and when water is applied it immediately runs out, take down the basket and immerse it in water. When bubbles cease to rise from the compost, remove the basket and let excess water drain. If plants have become damaged through lack of water, remove wilted flowers.

Window boxes

Window boxes displayed on sills outside sash windows can be watered from inside, and this is ideal for upstairs windows. Window boxes on brackets positioned beneath windows are easier to water from outside. Whenever possible, use proprietary extension fittings to hosepipes so that the job of watering is safe. You should never stand on a box in order to get greater height.

Pots

Where pots are clustered together, the task of watering is made easier by tying the end of a hosepipe to a cane. Slowly dribble water onto the compost; when pots have been newly planted, the compost is easily disturbed by fierce jets of water.

Where shrubs and small trees are planted in clay pots, it is possible to judge if water is required by tapping the pot with a wooden bobbin attached to the end of a bamboo cane. If, when tapped, the pot emits a ringing note, water is needed, whereas if a dull note is produced, this indicates that the compost is sufficiently moist already.

FEEDING PLANTS

HANGING-BASKETS	WINDOW BOXES, WALL-BASKETS, AND MANGERS	TUBS, POTS AND PLANTERS
These are invariably planted with summer-flowering plants and their display is from late spring to early autumn. Foliage plants are often added to the display. Therefore, feeding every two weeks throughout summer is essential.	*These become homes for many different types of plants throughout the year. During summer, they have the same types of plants as hanging-baskets and can be watered and fed in the same way.*	*Tubs, pots and planters create homes for many different types of plants and this influences their feeding needs.*

HANGING-BASKETS

- The easiest and best way is to add a liquid fertilizer to the water when watering. By this method, roots throughout the basket will be fed. Always water the basket immediately before applying a liquid fertilizer. Never use a fertilizer on dry compost because this may burn and damage the roots of the plants.
- Sometimes, pellets and fertilizer sticks are used, but these tend to cause roots to develop unevenly throughout the container, which may be to the detriment of some plants.

WINDOW BOXES, WALL-BASKETS, AND MANGERS

- They also create exciting displays in spring, from bulbs and hardy biennials such as double Daisies and Polyanthus. These plants are put in place in autumn and do not need any feeding; bulbs are nature's storehouses of energy.
- Window boxes also have winter displays, which are usually formed of late winter-flowering bulbs, small evergreen shrubs, conifers, and trailing plants such as variegated small-leaved *Hedera helix* (Ivies). None of these plants will need feeding, unless they are to be left in a window box for a long time.

TUBS, POTS AND PLANTERS

- Where ephemeral, summer-flowering plants are planted in pots and planters —and especially when in peat-based compost—regular feeding throughout summer is essential to maintain an attractive display.
- Where plants with a more permanent nature are used—and especially when planted in loam-based compost— regular feeding is not so necessary.
- When long-term plants such as shrubs and small trees are used in tubs and large pots, in spring remove about 1 inch of surface soil—without damaging roots—and replace with fresh compost.

DEADHEADING PLANTS

Unsightly dead flowerhead

Hold the main stem firmly, while bending over and snapping off the stem of a dead flowerhead. Place it on a garbage heap.

Regularly removing dead flowers encourages the development of further blooms. Additionally, if dead flowers are left on plants, they encourage the presence of diseases, which might spread throughout all of the plants. Some flowers have a mass of small flowers and these need to be removed individually by either pulling or twisting them sideways. Other flowers, such as Pelargoniums, have clustered flowers attached to a single stalk. Either snap the stem sideways or use scissors or a sharp knife.

ENCOURAGING BUSHINESS

Some plants have a natural, bushy habit and do not have to be encouraged to develop masses of stems. They have stems which arise from leaf-joints without anything being done to the plant. Other plants need to have their terminal shoots, or growing tips, removed.

Fuchsias, when young, benefit from having shoots nipped off to just above a leaf-joint. This encourages the development of further shoots; it may need to be done several times. It is essential to nip shoots back to just above a leaf-joint; if long, bare, pieces of stem are left, they will decay and die back.

Pinch out the tip between finger and thumb

Nipping off a growing tip encourages the growth of sideshoots lower down.

COPING WITH LATE FROSTS

Late spring frosts soon damage young, tender shoots on summer-flowering plants. Some plants, such as those grown in hanging-baskets, are especially at risk and if a frost is forecast, a few sheets of newspaper pushed over the plants and between the supporting chains will be helpful. However, if a severe frost is forecast, put the entire basket in a frostproof greenhouse or shed. Summer-flowering plants in window boxes are also at risk and these can also be protected by a few sheets of newspaper. Protecting tender evergreen shrubs from severe frost is described on page 74, as well as preventing the compost becoming saturated with water, freezing and damaging the roots.

Protect plants from the danger of late frosts by placing a few sheets of newspaper over them.

Plants in window boxes also need protection from frost by covering with newspaper.

Winter protection

Is winter protection important?

Many slightly tender shrubs and trees can be grown in temperate climates if given protection from frost and sudden dips in temperature during winter. Deciduous shrubs and trees shed their leaves in autumn and overwinter as bare stems and branches, but evergreen types are more at risk and these are the ones that especially need protection. Small ones can be moved into a frostproof greenhouse or lobby. Cloaking them in straw is an alternative.

PROTECTING TENDER EVERGREENS

Whether tender shrubs or trees are growing in tubs, large pots, or Versailles planters, they all can be protected by cloaking the foliage in straw. As soon as the temperature falls and frost is forecast, cloak and protect all your tender shrubs and trees. Clearly, the need to protect a plant depends on the local climate. Exposure to coastal areas—some engulfed in warm water, others known for their cold temperatures—can also have an influence. Throughout the winter, regularly check the straw and remove it as soon as the weather starts to improve. If it is left in position too long, there may be a risk of the plant being damaged when growth resumes.

1 *Insert about five 5-foot long pliable canes about 5 inches deep in compost close to the tub's edge. Gently pull the tops of the canes together to form a wigwam, so that they cross 6–8 inches from the top. Use strong string to hold them together and, if possible, flex and bend the canes outward so that all the plant's foliage is within their area. If a few young shoots extend outward it is not usually a problem, as later they can be covered in a layer of straw.*

2 *Starting from the top of the wigwam of canes, spread a thick layer of straw evenly over the entire surface. It is usually necessary to push straw between a few canes, so that it is temporarily held in place. As an alternative to straw, you can use hay, but this is not as weather-resistant as straw. Secure the end of a ball of string to the top and start winding downward, in a slight spiral. Add further straw as the spiral proceeds. Continue adding straw until the bottom is reached, when the end of the string can be tied to a cane.*

Problems with snow

A flurry and light coating of snow on leaves of evergreen shrubs is usually not a problem; it can be easily dusted off with a soft brush or a branch tapped with a cane to remove it. Essentially, it must be removed before it freezes and subsequent falls of snow build up on it, causing branches to become weighed down and, eventually, misshapen.

Bamboos chosen for growing in containers are usually sufficiently hardy to withstand cold weather in temperate climates, but heavy snowfalls bend the canes over and, if not removed, cause them to become misshapen.

PROTECTING COMPOST

Compost in tubs and large pots is at risk of becoming too wet during the winter months. Plants are not active and excessive water damages the compost and the plant's roots, especially when frozen. Therefore, in late autumn place two bricks on the compost (above) to ensure that water drains away. Cover the compost with plastic sheeting (right). Remove it in late winter.

PROTECTING CONTAINERS

Some containers—such as those formed of thin plastic or glass-fiber—give little protection to compost in containers during winter and consequently soil balls and roots are at risk. Thin metal containers, although having a trendy and modern appearance, also put roots at risk. Cloaking these containers in sacking that encapsulates straw gives protection, but, if soaked in rain which then freezes, acts like a refrigerator, so keep a careful eye on weather conditions and be ready to take the container under cover temporarily (see below).

Storing pots and tubs in winter

Winter plays havoc with containers and, wherever possible, you should store them under cover. If this is not possible, it is a good idea to cover them with polyethylene to prevent water penetrating them. It is a combination of water and freezing temperatures that causes most trouble, although water at any time of year puts wood at risk.

Fixing brackets and hooks

General deterioration, strong wind, and weak and crumbling brickwork makes brackets that support hanging-baskets, window boxes, and other wall-mounted containers at risk of failing and causing damage to plants and people. Yearly, in autumn or spring and before putting containers in place, check that fixings are secure and that brackets are strong enough for another season. Never take risks as displays could be ruined and someone severely injured.

How strong should the fixings be?

GETTING THE FIXINGS RIGHT

Using secure fixings in walls is absolutely essential; two of the best types to use are illustrated below:

For fixing to wallboard, perhaps in a porch or lobby

For fixing to brick walls, outdoors and indoors

POSITIONING HANGING-BASKETS

Practical positions

✔ Against walls and on wide patios and terraces.

✔ Where passers-by cannot knock them with their heads or shoulders.

✔ Where they will not be buffeted by strong winds that damage plants and loosen supporting brackets.

Impractical positions

✘ Alongside narrow paths and where water can drip onto plants and people passing beneath.

✘ Where plants are difficult to reach for watering and routine care.

✘ Where the basket over-hangs a sidewalk.

SECURING HANGING-BASKETS

Securing cup-hooks to bargeboards or fascias: this is only practical on one-storied houses, where the eaves extend 15 inches beyond the brickwork of the house walls. Additionally, it is only possible where the bargeboard or fascia is made of strong wood, rather than of plastic or wallboard. Always use strong cup-hooks for this purpose.

Securing brackets to wooden walls: some homes are constructed of a wooden framework, with the addition of wooden or plastic cladding. When securing a bracket, check that the desired position is structurally sound and able to give support. Use an awl to mark the position, and use a thin drill to provide the screw with guidance and to prevent the wood being strained by the width of the screw. Nevertheless, the fixing must be quite secure.

Supporting chains: where possible—and especially for large, outdoor hanging-baskets—use hanging-baskets that are suspended from four chains rather than three. Then, each spring, check that the chains are strong and not corroded and weakened. Also remember to inspect the hooks that secure them to the basket and hook at the top.

FIXING WINDOW BOX BRACKETS

When fixing window box brackets to a wall they must be strong, secure, attractive, level, and positioned centrally under a window. On casement windows, their distance beneath a sill is important to enable the window to open freely over plants.

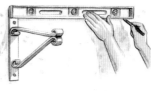

1 *First, measure down from the sill and mark on the wall the top of the first bracket—the depth of the windowbox plus 5–8 inches. Position the brackets so that the box will be supported about one-third in from each side, yet in the middle of the window.*

2 *Mark the drilling positions on the wall and, using a masonry drill, make the holes. Push one of the wall-anchors into each hole and then use galvanized, round-headed screws to hold the bracket firmly in the correct place.*

3 *Hold the other bracket in place (an equal distance in from the other side of the window) and, using a builder's spirit-level, mark the drilling holes. Insert wall-anchors and screw the bracket in place. Check that the window box will not be able to fall forward and off the brackets (most brackets have lipped edges).*

CRIME-BUSTING

There are security devices available that prevent hanging-baskets and their displays being stolen. Alternatively, twist some strong wire around the supporting hook.

SAFETY WITH POWER DRILLS

When using a power drill, always check that there is a GFCI installed that will instantly cut off the power should a electrical short be created.

Pests and diseases

How do I keep my container plants healthy?

Hanging-baskets, window boxes, and wall-baskets, as well as pots and tubs, become packed with tender plants during summer, creating succulent feasts for pests. They are also excellent places for diseases. Some pests, such as snails, slugs, woodlice, and earwigs, have a crawling nature, while others fly and soon spread damage from one container to another. Vigilance is essential, and when watering and looking after plants, check that pests and diseases are not present—and take control measures immediately.

Cyclamen mites

Often seen on Cyclamen and Pelargoniums indoors, and therefore occasionally in hanging-baskets in lobbies. **Pick off infected leaves or destroy severely infested plants.**

Red spider mites

These sometimes infest plants in lobbies. They suck sap, causing bleached areas. **Increase ventilation, mist-spray leaves, and spray with a systemic insecticide.**

Gray mold

Often known as botrytis, this creates fluffy, mold-like growths on flowers and soft stems. **Cut off and destroy infected plants. Increase ventilation and use a fungicide.**

Viruses

These infect many plants, causing discoloration and distortion. Leaves may have white streaks. **There is no cure: throw away and burn badly infected plants and spray with insecticides to kill sucking pests such as aphids that spread them.**

Caterpillars

They chew soft leaves and stems, making them unsightly. **Pick off caterpillars as soon as they are seen—and destroy. Additionally, spray plants with an insecticide at ten-day intervals. At the end of summer, pull up and burn all decayed material to prevent infestations during the following year.**

Powdery mildew

This sometimes coats leaves with a white, powdery deposit. It is occasionally seen on plants indoors, so check plants in lobbies. **Pick off infected leaves, improve ventilation, and spray with a fungicide.**

Woodlice

They climb walls and infest wall-baskets and window boxes, as well as plants in pots, tubs, and growing-bags on a patio. They mainly come out of hiding at night and chew leaves, stems, flowers, and roots. **Dust with an insecticide.**

Whitefly

These are small, white, moth-like insects that flutter from one plant to another, sucking sap and causing mottling. **Spray with an insecticide. Control is difficult.**

SAFETY FIRST

Chemicals sprayed on plants in gardens and lobbies are lethal to pests and therefore must be treated with a great deal of respect.

- Carefully follow the manufacturer's directions. Don't be tempted to use chemicals at a higher than recommended concentration as they will not be more effective—and may even damage plants.
- Don't mix two different chemicals, unless recommended.
- Before using, check that the chemical will not damage specific plants.
- Keep all chemicals away from children and pets. Don't transfer chemicals into bottles that children might believe to contain a refreshing drink.
- Don't use the same equipment for both weedkillers and insecticides.
- Thoroughly wash all spraying equipment after use.

Thrips

These infest plants in lobbies and porches, where they hop and flit from one plant to another. They cause streaking and mottling. **Use an insecticide.**

Aphids (greenfly)

These are pernicious pests that suck sap, causing mottling and distortion. Blackfly sometimes infest plants, especially nasturtiums. **Spray plants with an insecticide every 10–14 days throughout summer.**

Earwigs

These are pernicious pests, hiding during the day and chewing and tearing leaves, flowers, and soft stems at night. They attack plants in window boxes and wall-baskets, as well as in hanging-baskets if they can be reached. **Pick off and destroy them; also spray with an insecticide.**

Snails

They have similar appetites to slugs, and infest plants in the same way. **Pick them off and use baits and traps.**

Slugs

These are nature's stealth pests; they hide during the day and come out at night to decimate plants in tubs, pots, growing-bags, and other containers on patios. They also climb walls to get at plants in window boxes and wall-baskets. **Pick them off and destroy them. It is also possible to use baits and traps, such as saucers filled with beer and sugar. Take care, however, that domestic pets, as well as wild animals such as hedgehogs, cannot reach the baits or traps.**

Glossary

Annual
A plant that is raised from seed and completes its life cycle within one growing season. Some annuals are half-hardy in temperate zones and therefore raised in gentle warmth in late winter or early spring. They are planted into containers in late spring or early summer, when all risk of frost has passed.

Barrels
Wooden containers used during earlier years to transport all manner of materials, including beer, flour, tobacco, and gunpowder. They range from a pin (4½ gallons) to a butt (108 gallons). Today, barrels are either cut in half to form tubs, or left intact and drilled so that plants such as strawberries can be grown in them.

Biennial
A plant that takes two growing seasons to grow from seed and to produce flowers. Many spring-flowering plants grown in containers are biennial, such as Wallflowers and Daisies.

Bulb
Formed of overlapping, fleshy, modified leaves, creating a food-storage organ that, when given the right conditions, develops leaves and flowers. Many spring-flowering plants in containers are bulbs, including Hyacinths and Daffodils.

Courtyards
Originally, open areas surrounded by buildings or walls, perhaps inside a castle. Nowadays, they are paved areas at the rear of a building and surrounded by a wall.

Crocks
Pieces of broken clay pots used to cover drainage holes in containers. They are placed concave side downwards.

Deadheading
The removal of faded flowers to encourage the development of further blooms.

Drip-tray
Integral with plastic-type hanging-baskets to prevent water dripping on floors and plants beneath.

Growing-bag
Originally introduced to grow tomatoes on disease-infected soil, but now widely used as homes for many flowering plants, as well as herbs and vegetables.

Herbaceous perennials
Plants that die down to soil level in autumn and send up fresh shoots in spring. Some of these can be grown in tubs and other large containers on a patio.

Jardinière
A large, decorative stand or pot that is used to display plants.

Loam-based compost
Formed mainly of fertile topsoil, with the addition of sharp sand, peat, and fertilizers.

Manger
Similar to a wire-framed wall-basket, but with a wider metal framework.

Patio
The Spanish used this term to describe an inner court, open to the sky and surrounded by a building. The term was introduced by the Spanish to North America, where it became to mean any paved area around a dwelling.

Peat-based compost
Formed mainly of peat, with the addition of fertilizers.

Perlite
A moisture-retentive material added to compost.

Reconstituted stone
Used to construct a wide range of plant containers and ornaments. It mellows to a pleasing color.

Reused growing-bags
Growing-bags which have been used for one season and, during a following season, topped up with peat and fertilizers and again used to grow plants.

Sink gardens
An unusual way to grow small plants such as miniature conifers, alpine plants and bulbs. Stone sinks are best, but modified glazed types can also be used.

Sphagnum moss
A type of moss, earlier and widely used to line wire-framed hanging-baskets to assist in moisture retention and to prevent compost spilling out of the container.

Terraces
Open, paved areas immediately outside a house. Sometimes, they are on several levels and united by flights of steps. Usually they have a firm, hard surface, but earlier long and large ones were grassed.

Terra-cotta
A hardy, brownish-red material formed of clay, fine sand, and, occasionally, pulverized pottery waste. This is made into containers—usually unglazed—for plants.

Urn
A vase of varying shape and ornamentation made of glass-fiber, metal, plastic, or reconstituted stone. Because of the limited amount of compost they can hold, they are mainly used for summer-flowering plants.

Veranda
A term derived from India, describing a gallery at ground level and on one side of a house (occasionally completely surrounding it). The roof is sloped to shed water and the sides are partly or wholly open on the garden side.

Versailles planter
A large, square-sided container originated at Versailles, France. Early ones were made of lead or slate, while modern types are usually made of glass-fiber or wood.

Vermiculite
A moisture-retentive material added to compost.

Index

Abies 35
Acer palmatum 32, 37
Adam's Needle, Variegated 33
Aegopodium podagraria 24
African Daisy 28
Agapanthus 24, 25
Agave americana 'Variegata' 24
Ageratum houstonianum 16
Ajuga reptans 24
Alchemilla mollis 24
Alcoves 69
Allium schoenoprasum 40
Anagallis
    A. linifolia 21
    A. monelli 16
Anemone blanda 39
Anthemis punctata cupaniana 25
Antirrhinum pendula multiflora 21
Aphids 77
Apples 6, 48, 49
Aquilegia McKana Hybrids 25
Argyranthemum frutescens 13
Arrow Bamboo 36
Asarina purpusii 'Victoria Falls' 16
Asarina x hybrida 'Red Dragon' 16
Asparagus densiflorus 7, 12, 13, 44, 45
Asplenium bulbiferum 7, 44
Astilbe x arendsii 25
Aucuba japonica 'Variegata' 11, 23, 32
Azaleas 30

Backgrounds 12–13
Balcony gardening 3
Balm 40
Bamboos 7, 36
Barrels 66, 71
Barrenwort 26
Basket Vine 45
Bassia scoparia 'Trichophylla' 11
Bay 40
Beans 46
Bedding plants 6, 16–21, 22–3
Bee Balm 28
Begonias 3, 11, 13
    B. semperflorens 16
    B. sutherlandii 17
    B. x tuberhybrida 17, 44, 45
Bellis perennis 10, 12, 22, 23
Berberis thunbergii 'Aurea' 33
Bergenia cordifolia 25
Bidens ferulifera 'Golden Eye' 17
Biennials 22
Bishop's Hat 26
Bishop's Weed 24
Black-stemmed Bamboo 36
Blazing Star 27
Bleeding Heart 25
Blueberries 48, 49
Blue Lungwort 27
Blue Passion Flower 43
Blue Pimpernel 16
Bonsai 37
Border plants 6
Box 14
Brachycombe iberidifolia 21
Brackets, fixing 75
Broom 31
Bubbling urn feature 67
Bulbs 7, 14, 38–9
Burning Bush 11
Bushiness, encouraging 73
Buxus sempervirens 14
Buying plants 50–1

Calceolaria integrifolia 17
Calceolaria x herbeohybrida 12, 13, 45
Calendula officinalis 17
California Poppy 18
Callisia elegans 45
Calluna vulgaris 33

Camellia x williamsii 30
Campanula
    C. carpatica 21
    C. isophylla 7, 12, 13, 17, 44
Canary Bird Flower 43
Canary Creeper 43
Capsicums 46, 47
Carex elata 'Aurea' 7
Caring for plants 72–3
Carpet Bugle 24
Casks 71
Castor Oil Plant 32
Caterpillars 76
Cathedral Bells 42
Century Plant, Variegated 24
Chamaecyparis
    C. lawsoniana 11, 34, 35
    C. obtusa 15
    C. pisifera 15, 34
Chemical safety 77
Cherry Pie 18
Chilean Glory Flower 42
Chinese Honeysuckle, Yellow-leaved 33
Chinese Windmill Palm 32, 33
Chionodoxa
    C. gigantea 38
    C. luciliae 39
Chives 40
Chlorophytum comosum 44, 45
Choisya ternata 30, 32
Choosing plants 50–1
Christmas Rose 26
Chrysanthemums 13, 44
Clematis 7, 15, 17, 42, 43
Climbers 7, 15, 42–3
Clockvine 20, 43
Cobaea scandens 42
Colors, harmonizing 12–13
Common Houseleek 29
Compost
    in barrels and casks 71
    in hanging-baskets 53, 55
    in lobbies and porches 57
    protecting from winter 74
    in sinks 61
    in troughs and planters 62
    in wall-baskets and mangers 59
    in water features 66
Concrete containers 5
Conifers 7, 11, 15, 34–5
Coral Bells 27
Coral Flower 27
Cordylines 32, 33
Corms 38–9
Cranesbill 26
Creeping Jenny 11, 13, 16, 28
Crocosmia x crocosmiiflora 25
Crocuses 10, 13, 14, 23, 38
Cucumbers 46
Cup-and-Saucer Vine 42
Cyclamen mites 76
Cypress 15

Daffodils 10, 38, 39, 65
English Daisies 10, 12, 22, 23
Dark backgrounds 13
Datura 'Ballerina Mixed' 18
Datura meteloides 18
Day Lily 26
Deadheading 73
Dead Nettle 27
Dicentra spectabilis 25
Diseases 76–7
Displays
    creating tripod 42
    harmonizing 12–13
    seasonal 10, 23, 53, 59
Doronicums 26
Doronicum hirsutum 31
Dracaena 45
Drainage 5
Drill safety 75

Earthenware pots 5
Earwigs 76, 77
Eastern Red Cedar 15
Eccremocarpus scaber 42
Eggplants 46
Elaeagnus pungens 'Maculata' 32
Electric drill safety 75
Elephant's Ears 25
Epimedium perralderianum 26
Eranthis hyemalis 39
Ericas 11, 31
Erysimums 10, 12, 22
Eschscholzia maritima prostrata 18
Eucalyptus gunnii 33
Euonymus fortunei 23, 32

Fagus sylvatica 37
False Castor Oil Plant 32, 33
Fargesias 36
Fatsia japonica 32, 33
Feeding 55, 57, 59, 61, 73
Ferns 7, 12, 13, 44
Ficus radicans 'Variegata' 45
Figs 49
Fixing brackets 75
Florist's Cineraria 45
Floss Flower 16
Foam Flower 29
Foliage 12
Forget-me-nots 10, 12, 22, 23
Forsythia 37
Fountain Bamboo 36
Foxtail Fern 44
Fragrance 14–15
Frosts 73
Fruit 48–9
Fuchsias 13, 31

Galanthus nivalis 38
Garden centers 50
Gaultheria procumbens 11
Spike Gayfeather 27
Genista pilosa 'Vancouver Gold' 31
Geraniums 16, 17, 26, 27, 45
Ginkgo biloba 37
Glory Flower 42
Glory of the Snow 38, 39
Gold Dust Plant 32
Golden Balm 28
Golden-haired Bamboo 36
Golden Marguerite 25
Granny's Bonnet 25
Grape Hyacinth 10, 13, 23, 39, 59
Grasses 28
Green, influence of 12
Greenfly 77
Gray mold 76
Gray-stone backgrounds 12
Ground Elder 24
Growing-bags 5, 9, 47, 68
Gypsophila muralis 'Gypsy' 21

Hakonechloa macra 'Aureola' 26
Hanging-baskets 4, 9, 11, 51, 54–7
Hardy biennials 22
Hardy border plants 6
Harmonizing displays 12–13
Harvesting herbs 40–1
Healthy plants 50
Heaths 11, 31
Hebe
    H. 'Margret' 31
    H. pinguifolia 'Pagei' 33
    H. x andersoniana 23, 33
    H. x franciscana 33
Hedera helix 11, 13, 23, 45
Helichrysum petiolare 13, 16, 45
Heliotrope 14, 18
Helleborus 26
Hemerocallis 26, 27
Herbs 7, 9, 40–1, 65
Heuchera sanguinea 27

Hollyhocks 22
Honeysuckle, Yellow-leaved Chinese 33
Hooks, fixing 75
Hop, Yellow-leaved 7, 42
Hostas 26, 27
Houttuynia cordata 'Chameleon' 27
Humulus lupulus 'Aureus' 7, 42
Hyacinths 10, 12, 13, 14, 15, 39
Hydrangea macrophylla 31
Hypericum 31
Hypertufa sinks 61

Ice Plant 29
Impatiens 11, 18, 21
Ipheion uniflora 39
Ipomoea tricolor 42
Irises 10, 14, 23, 39
Italian Bellflower 7, 12, 13, 17, 44
Ivies 11, 13, 23, 45

Japanese Maple 37
Japanese Spurge, Variegated 28
Japanese White Pine 37
Japanese Wisteria 37
Jardinières 5
Jasmine 15
Jerusalem Sage 29
Juniperus
    J. chinensis 34
    J. communis 34, 35
    J. horizontalis 11, 35
    J. scopularium 35
    J. squamata 35
    J. virginiana 15
    J. x pfitzeriana 35

Knotweed 29

Lady's Mantle 24
Lamb's Tongue 29
Lamiums 27
Lathyrus odoratus 43
Laurentia axillaris Stars Series 18
Laurus nobilis 40
Lavandula angustifolia 'Hidcote' 31
Lavender Cotton 14
Lenten Rose 26
Leopard's Bane 26
Lettuces 7, 9, 47
Leucojum vernum 39
Liatris spicata 27
Licorice Plant 13, 16, 45
Light 12
Ligustrum ovalifolium 'Aureum' 33
Lilies 15, 24, 26, 38
Limonium latifolium 27
Lobbies 7, 44–5, 56–7
Lobelias 11, 12, 18, 45
Lobularia maritima 11, 14, 18, 19
Lonicera
    L. americana 15
    L. nitida 'Baggeson's Gold' 33
Lysimachia nummularia 11, 13, 16, 28

Magnolia stellata 31
Mahonia 'Charity' 31
Mail order 50
Malcolmia maritima 15
Malus baccata 37
Mangers 8, 58–9
Marguerites 13
Marigolds 12, 17, 20
Marjoram 41
Matthiola
    M. bicornis 15
    M. incana 12, 13
Melissa officinalis 28, 40
Mentha spicata 40
Metake 36
Mexican Orange Blossom, Yellow-leaved 32
Mexican Orange Flower 30

Miniature ponds 3
Mint 40, 41
Moisture retention 55
Monarda didyma 28
Moneywort 28
Moneywort, Yellow-leaved 28
Montbretia 25
Morning Glory 42
Mother Fern 44
Muscari armeniacum 10, 13, 23, 39, 59
Myosotis 10, 12, 22, 23

Nandina domestica 33
Nasturtiums 12, 13, 14, 20, 43
Nemophylla
    N. maculata 21
    N. menziesii 21
Nephrolepis exaltata 44
New Zealand Flax 28
New Zealand Hemp 28
Nicotiana 14, 19
Nierembergia 'Mont Blanc' 21
Nurseries 50

Oplismenus hirtellus 'Variegatus' 45
Origanum majorana 41
Osteospermum ecklonis prostratum 28
Oswego Tea 28

Pachysandra terminalis 'Variegata' 28
Pansies 11, 14, 19
Parsley 41
Passiflora caerulea 43
Passion Flower 43
Patience Plants 11, 18
Patios 68
Peaches 49
Pebble ponds 3
Pelargoniums 11, 16, 19, 27, 45
Pellaea rotundifolia 44
Perennials 22, 24–9
Pericallis x hybrida 45
Periwinkles 23
Pests 76–7
Petroselinum crispum 41
Petunias 13, 19, 45
Phormiums 28, 29
Phyllostachys
    P. aurea 36
    P. nigra 36
Piggy-back Plant 29, 45
Pinus
    P. parviflora 37
    P. sylvestris 35, 37
Plantain Lily 27
Plant care 72–3
Planters 5, 62
Planting 51, 55, 57, 59, 61, 65
Pleioblastus
    P. pygmaeus 36

P. variegatus 36
P. viridistriatus 36
Plunging pots 53
Pockets, planting 69
Polyanthus 10, 22, 23
Polygonum affine 'Dimity' 29
Ponds 3
Porches 7, 44–5, 56–7
Positioning containers 8–9
Positioning hanging-baskets 75
Potatoes 7, 47, 68
Pots 8, 51, 64–5
Pouch Flower 17, 45
Pouch gardening 69
Powdery mildew 76
Preparing sinks 60
Primula x polyantha 22
Problems, plant 50, 76–7
Prunus incisa 'Kojo Nomal' 31
Pseudosasa japonica 36
Pulmonaria officinalis 29
Pussy-foot 16

Queen of the Arundinarias 36

Radishes 47
Raised beds 63
Red-brick backgrounds 13
Red spider mites 76
Rhododendron yakushimanum 31
Ricinus communis 32
Rock Bell 21
Rosemary 14, 30, 31, 41
Roses 15, 30
Rue 41
Ruta graveolens 41

Safety with chemicals 77
Sage 14, 32, 41
Salix babylonica 37
Salvia
    S. officinalis 14, 32, 41
    S. splendens 19
Sambucus racemosa 33
Santolina chamaecyparissus 14
Sanvitalia procumbens 20
Saxifraga stolonifera 'Tricolor' 45
Scarlet Sage 19
Scent 14–15
Schoenoplectus lacustris tabernaemontani 7
Sea Lavender 27
Securing hanging-baskets 75
Sedum 29, 45
Selecting plants 25
Semiarundinaria fastuosa 36
Sempervivum tectorum 29
Senecio cineraria 'Silver Dust' 16
Shelves, planting 69
Shrubby Veronica 31, 33
Shrubs 6, 11, 30, 32–3
Silene pendula 'Peach Blossom' 21

Silvery Inch Plant 45
Sinks 9, 60–1, 66
Skimmias 11
Slipperwort 12, 13, 17
Slugs and snails 76, 77
Snow 74
Snowdrops 38
Snowflake 39
Sphagnum moss 55
Spider Plant 44
Spotted Laurel 23, 32
Spring displays 10, 12–13, 23, 53, 59
Stachys byzantina 29
Star Magnolia 31
Statice 27
Stenotaphrum secundatum 45
Stocks 12, 13, 15
Storing containers 74
Storing herbs 40–1
Strawberries 5, 6, 48, 49, 71
Striped Inch Plant 45
Summer displays 11, 12–13, 53, 59
Sweet Alyssum 11, 14, 18
Sweet Peas 7, 43
Sweet peppers 46, 47

Tagetes 12, 20
Tap water 72
Taxus baccata 'Standishii' 35
Temperature 4
Thamnocalamus 36
Thorn Apple 18
Thorny Elaeagnus, Variegated 32
Thrips 77
Thuja 35
Thunbergia alata 20, 43
Thyme 41
Tiarella cordifolia 29
Tobacco Plant 14, 19
Tolmiea menziesii 29, 45
Tomatoes 5, 7, 9, 46, 47, 68
Trachycarpus fortunei 32, 33
Trailing fig 45
Transporting plants 51
Trees 6
Tripod displays, creating 42
Tropaeolum majus 12, 14, 20, 43
Troughs 4, 8, 15, 51, 62
Tsuga heterophylla 37
Tubs 5, 8, 51, 64–5, 66
Tulips 10, 13, 23, 39, 59
Types of containers 4
Typha minima 7

Ulmus procera 37
Urns 5, 51, 64–5

Variegated Adam's Needle 33
Variegated Century Plant 24
Variegated Japanese Spurge 28
Variegated Thorny Elaeagnus 32
Vegetables 7, 46–7

Verbena
    V. erinoides 'Lavender Mist' 20
    V. x hybrida 'Sandy Mixed' 20
Vinca major 23
Vinca minor 'Variegata' 23
Viola
    V. x hybrida 21
    V. x williamsiana 21
    V. x wittrockiana 11, 14, 21
Viruses 76

Wahlenbergia annularis 21
Wall-baskets 8, 13, 15, 58–9
Wallflowers 10, 12, 22
Wall-mask waterspout 67
Water butts 72
Water features 3, 66–7
Water-garden plants 7, 67
Water gardens, miniature 5, 9
Watering 55, 57, 59, 61, 72
Waterlilies 67
Weeping Willow 37
Wheelbarrows, decorative 9, 70
White backgrounds 12
Whitefly 77
Window boxes 4, 8, 10–11, 51, 52–3
Winter Aconite 39
Winter displays 53
Winter protection 74
Wisteria 15, 37, 43
Wooden planters 51, 65
Woodlice 76

Yellow-leaved Chinese Honeysuckle 33
Yellow-leaved Hop 7, 42
Yellow-leaved Mexican Orange Blossom 32
Yellow-leaved Moneywort 28
Youth and Old Age 21, 45
Yuccas 32, 33

Zebra Rush 7
Zebrina pendula 45
Zelkova serrata 37
Zinnias 12, 13, 21
Zucchini 46

Acknowledgments

AG&G Books would like to thank the following suppliers for their contribution: **B&Q plc**, Head Office, Portswood House, 1 Hampshire Corporate Park, Chandlers Ford, Eastleigh, Hampshire SO53 3YX, UK, Tel: 01703 256256, **Barbary Pots**, www.barbarypots.co.uk, **Forest Garden plc (Builder Center)**, www.forestgarden.co.uk, **Thompson & Morgan**, Quality Seedsmen Since 1855, *brings the finest quality flower and vegetable seed and flower plant varieties to the home gardener,* Thompson & Morgan (UK) Ltd, Poplar Lane, Ipswich, Suffolk, IP8 3BU, **Windowbox.com**, www.windowbox.com. Photographs: AG&G Books (cover and pages 2, 3, 12, 43CL, 47BL, 50, 52TL AND WINDOWBOXES: PAINTED PINE, DECORATED WOOD, TERRACOTTA AND PLASTIC LEAD EFFECT, 54, 56, 58, 60, 61, 62 EXCEPT TL, 63, 64 POT ETC OPTIONS: ALL PICTURES EXCEPT THOSE LISTED HERE, 65, 69 and 70), B&Q (page 64 POT ETC OPTIONS: LARGE PLASTIC POT, TERRACOTTA 'LONG TOMS', FLARED-SHAPE TERRACOTTA POT, DECORATED GLAZED POT AND GLAZED CERAMIC POTS), Barbary Pots (page 64 POT ETC OPTIONS: LARGE HANDMADE TERRACOTTA URN AT CENTRE), Peter Chan (page 37BL, BC AND BR), John Douch (page 37CR), Forest Garden (pages 52 WINDOWBOXES: PINE LOG EFFECT AND LATTICE FRONT and 62TL), Garden Matters (pages 17CR AND BL, 34BL, 35CL and 44CR), Garden World Images (page 31TC AND TR), Peter McHoy (pages 16C, 18BR, 20TL, 22CR, 24C, 25BC, 26TL AND CR, 27CL, 28TL, TC AND CR, 29CR, BL AND BC, 32BL, 33TR AND C, 34CL, C AND CR, 35TL, TC, TR AND BL, 36CR, BL AND BC, 38BL, 39TL, TC, CL AND BL, 40C AND BR, 41TL, 42C, CR AND BR, 43BC, 44C, BC AND BR, 45TC, TR AND BC, 47C, 48BR and 49C AND BC), David Squire (all pictures except those listed here), Thompson & Morgan (pages 16CR, BL, BC AND BR, 17TL, TC, TR, BR, AND BC, 18TL, TC, TR, C, CR AND BL, 19 EXCEPT BC, 20TC, BC, BR, 21 EXCEPT CR, 22CL, 46, 47TC, CL AND BC) and Windowbox.com (page 52 WINDOWBOXES: CEDAR, METAL FRAME, WHITE-PAINTED STEEL, RECONSTITUTED STONE, PLASTIC KIT AND WOVEN WILLOW).